TEACHER'S PET PUBLICATIONS

LITPLAN TEACHER PACK
for
Johnny Tremain
based on the book by
Esther Forbes

Written by
Barbara Linde, M.A. Ed.

© 1996 Teacher's Pet Publications
All Rights Reserved

This **LitPlan** for Esther Forbes'
Johnny Tremain
has been brought to you by Teacher's Pet Publications, Inc.

Copyright Teacher's Pet Publications 1996
11504 Hammock Point
Berlin MD 21811

Only the student materials in this unit plan (such as worksheets,
study questions, and tests) may be reproduced multiple times
for use in the purchaser's classroom.

For any additional copyright questions,
contact Teacher's Pet Publications.

www.tpet.com

TABLE OF CONTENTS - *Johnny Tremain*

Introduction	5
Unit Objectives	7
Unit Outline	8
Reading Assignment Sheet	9
Study Questions	13
Quiz/Study Questions (Multiple Choice)	25
Pre-Reading Vocabulary Worksheets	43
Lesson One (Introductory Lesson)	49
Nonfiction Assignment Sheet	73
Oral Reading Evaluation Form	75
Writing Assignment 1	78
Writing Evaluation Form	79
Writing Assignment 2	83
Extra Writing Assignments/Discussion ?s	87
Writing Assignment 3	93
Vocabulary Review Activities	95
Unit Review Activities	96
Unit Tests	103
Unit Resource Materials	139
Vocabulary Resource Materials	155

A FEW NOTES ABOUT THE AUTHOR
ESTHER FORBES

Forbes, Esther (1891-1967), U. S. author, born on June 28, 1891, in Westborough, Mass. Forbes's historical works, both fiction and nonfiction, brought the lives of young people in early America to life for contemporary readers.

Forbes studied at Bradford Junior College and the University of Wisconsin. She served on the staff of Houghton Mifflin publishers in Boston from 1920 to 1926 and from 1942 to 1946. She received the Pulitzer prize in historian 1943 for 'Paul Revere and the World He Lived In' (1942). The book examines Revere both as an artisan and as a member of the New England community that was pivotal at the time of the American Revolution. Her other historical studies included 'A Mirror for Witches' (1928) and 'America's Paul Revere' (1946).

Forbes is perhaps best known for 'Johnny Tremain: A Novel for Young and Old" (1943), which won the 1944 Newbery Medal. The book was her only novel written for children. Her novels for adults included 'Paradise' (1937), 'The Running of the Tide' (1948), and 'Rainbow on the Road' (1959). 'The Running of the Tide', which was set in Salem before the War of 1812, was made into a motion picture after having won the Metro-Goldwyn-Mayer novel award. 'Johnny Tremain' became a favorite of students, teachers, and curious readers of all ages. The novel, which traces the development of a young orphan boy from his days as a silversmith's apprentice to his participation in the American Revolution, evolved from the author's research on Paul Revere. It was made into a motion picture by Walt Disney and into a television show. Forbes's novels were also translated into more than ten languages. Forbes was awarded honorary degrees from Clark University, the University of Maine, the University of Wisconsin, Northeastern University, Wellesley College, and Tufts University. She died on August 12, 1967, in Worcester, Mass.

Courtesy of Compton's Learning Company

INTRODUCTION

This unit has been designed to develop students' reading, writing, thinking, listening and speaking skills through exercises and activities related to *Johnny Tremain* by Esther Forbes. It includes twenty-three lessons, supported by extra resource materials.

The **introductory lesson** introduces students to one main theme of the novel *Johnny Tremain* through a bulletin board activity. Following the introductory activity, students are given an explanation of how the activity relates to the book they are about to read.

The **reading assignments** are approximately thirty pages each; some are a little shorter while others are a little longer. Students have approximately 15 minutes of pre-reading work to do prior to each reading assignment. This pre-reading work involves reviewing the study questions for the assignment and doing some vocabulary work for 8 to 10 vocabulary words they will encounter in their reading.

The **study guide questions** are fact-based questions; students can find the answers to these questions right in the text. These questions come in two formats: short answer or multiple choice. The best use of these materials is probably to use the short answer version of the questions as study guides for students (since answers will be more complete), and to use the multiple choice version for occasional quizzes. It might be a good idea to make transparencies of your answer keys for the overhead projector.

The **vocabulary work** is intended to enrich students' vocabularies as well as to aid in the students' understanding of the book. Prior to each reading assignment, students will complete a two-part worksheet for approximately 8 to 10 vocabulary words in the upcoming reading assignment. Part I focuses on students' use of general knowledge and contextual clues by giving the sentence in which the word appears in the text. Students are then to write down what they think the words mean based on the words' usage. Part II gives students dictionary definitions of the words and has them match the words to the correct definitions based on the words' contextual usage. Students should then have an understanding of the words when they meet them in the text.

After each reading assignment, students will go back and formulate answers for the study guide questions. Discussion of these questions serves as a **review** of the most important events and ideas presented in the reading assignments.

After students complete extra discussion questions, there is a **vocabulary review** lesson which pulls together all of the separate vocabulary lists for the reading assignments and gives students a review of all of the words they have studied.

Following the reading of the book, two lessons are devoted to the **extra discussion questions/writing assignments**. These questions focus on interpretation, critical analysis and personal response, employing a variety of thinking skills and adding to the students' understanding of the novel. These questions are done as a **group activity**. Using the information they have acquired so far through individual work and class discussions, students get together to further examine the text and to brainstorm ideas relating to the themes of the novel.

The group activity is followed by a **reports and discussion** session in which the groups share their ideas about the book with the entire class; thus, the entire class gets exposed to many different ideas regarding the themes and events of the book.

There are three **writing assignments** in this unit, each with the purpose of informing, persuading, or having students express personal opinions. The first assignment is to express a personal **opinion**: students will make a poster to show ways to help the handicapped. The second assignment is to **persuade**: students will take a position as a Whig or a Tory and persuade a friend to join their cause. The third assignment is to **inform**: students will write a news article for the *Boston Observer* and describe one of the historical events mentioned in the book.

In addition, there is a **nonfiction reading assignment**. Students are required to read a piece of nonfiction related in some way to *Johnny Tremain*. After reading their nonfiction pieces, students will fill out a worksheet on which they answer questions regarding facts, interpretation, criticism, and personal opinions. During one class period, students make **oral presentations** about the nonfiction pieces they have read. This not only exposes all students to a wealth of information, it also gives students the opportunity to practice **public speaking**.

The **review lesson** pulls together all of the aspects of the unit. The teacher is given four or five choices of activities or games to use which all serve the same basic function of reviewing all of the information presented in the unit.

The **unit test** comes in two formats: all multiple choice-matching-true/false or with a mixture of matching, short answer, and composition. As a convenience, two different tests for each format have been included.

There are additional **support materials** included with this unit. The **resource sections** include suggestions for an in-class library, crossword and word search puzzles related to the novel, and extra vocabulary worksheets. There is a list of **bulletin board ideas** which gives the teacher suggestions for bulletin boards to go along with this unit. In addition, there is a list of **extra class activities** the teacher could choose from to enhance the unit or as a substitution for an exercise the teacher might feel is inappropriate for his/her class. **Answer keys** are located directly after the **reproducible student materials** throughout the unit. The student materials may be reproduced for use in the teacher's classroom without infringement of copyrights. No other portion of this unit may be reproduced without the written consent of Teacher's Pet Publications, Inc.

UNIT OBJECTIVES
Johnny Tremain

1. Through reading *Johnny Tremain,* students will analyze characters and their situations to better understand the themes of the novel.

2. Students will demonstrate their understanding of the text on four levels: factual, interpretive, critical, and personal.

3. Students will practice reading aloud and silently to improve their skills in each area.

4. Students will enrich their vocabularies and improve their understanding of the novel through the vocabulary lessons prepared for use in conjunction with it.

5. Students will answer questions to demonstrate their knowledge and understanding of the main events and characters in *Johnny Tremain.*

6. Students will identify the characteristics of historical fiction and distinguish between the historical and fictional events presented in the novel.

7. Students will practice writing through a variety of writing assignments.

8. The writing assignments in this are geared to several purposes:
    a. To check the students' reading comprehension
    b. To make students think about the ideas presented by the novel
    c. To make students put those ideas into perspective
    d. To encourage critical and logical thinking
    e. To provide the opportunity to practice good grammar and improve students' use of the English language.

9. Students will read aloud, report, and participate in large and small group discussions to improve their public speaking and personal interaction skills.

UNIT OUTLINE - *Johnny Tremain*

1	2	3	4	5
Unit Intro Distribute Unit Materials PV I	Read I Study ?? I	PVR II Oral Reading Evaluation	Study ?? III PVR III	Study ?? III Writing Assignment #1
6	7	8	9	10
Quiz I, II, III PVR IV	Study ?? IV PVR V	Study ?? V PVR VI	Writing Conference	Study ?? VI PVR VII
11	12	13	14	15
Quiz IV, V, VI, VII Study ?? VIII PVR IX	Writing Assignment #2	Study ?? IX PVR X	Study ?? X PVR XI	Study ?? XI PVR XII
16	17	18	19	20
Extra Discussion ??	Writing Assignment #3	Library Work	Movie/ Audio Cassette and Discussion	Non-Fiction Assignment
21	22	23		
Vocabulary Review	Review	Test		

Key: P = Preview Study Questions   V = Vocabulary Work   R = Read

READING ASSIGNMENT SHEET
Johnny Tremain

Date to be Assigned	Chapters	Completion Date
		(Prior to class on this date)
	Chapter I Up and About	
	Chapter II The Pride of Your Power	
	Chapter III An Earth of Brass	
	Chapter IV The Rising Eye	
	Chapter V *The Boston Observer*	
	Chapter VI Salt-Water Tea	
	Chapter VII The Fiddler's Bill	
	Chapter VIII A World to Come	
	Chapter IX The Scarlet Deluge	
	Chapter X 'Disperse, Ye Rebels'	
	Chapter XI Yankee Doodle	
	Chapter XII A Man Can Stand Up	

STUDY QUESTIONS

Study Questions *Johnny Tremain*

Chapter I Up and About

1. What is the setting of the novel?
2. What is Johnny's job?
3. How does Johnny get along with Dove and Dusty, and how do they feel about him?
4. Why did Mr. Lapham have Johnny read the Bible verses?
5. Which rich merchant came to the shop and why?
6. What did Johnny tell Cilla about his middle name and his childhood?

Chapter II The Pride of Your Power

1. To whom did Johnny go for help with the sugar basin? What was the result?
2. What problem did Johnny encounter with completing the sugar basin? What did he do about it?
3. Describe Johnny's accident, including who was responsible for it, and what the result was.
4. Describe Mrs. Lapham's treatment of Johnny after the accident.
5. What did Mr. Lapham tell Johnny after the accident?

Chapter III An Earth of Brass

1. Describe Johnny's method of looking for work. Was it effective?
2. Who was Percival Tweedie and why was he important?
3. Describe Johnny's first encounter with Rab.
4. How did Johnny's looks and dress change after the accident?
5. Describe Isannah's reaction when Johnny tried to pick her up in his arms. How did Johnny feel about it?

Chapter IV The Rising Eye

1. What did Mr. Jonathan Lyte think of Johnny's story at first? What did he do after Johnny described the cup?
2. Describe Johnny's visit to the Lyte mansion.
3. How did Rab help Johnny while he was in jail?
4. Why was Cilla's testimony important?
5. Describe the main events and outcome of the trial.

Study Questions *Johnny Tremain* Page 2

Chapter V *The Boston Observer*

1. How did Rab get Cilla to court?
2. What did Johnny do with his cup, and what was the result?
3. What job did Johnny take?
4. How did Johnny feel about his job?
5. What were the chairs in the attic at the Boston Observer used for?
6. How did Johnny, under Rab's guidance, begin to change, and what were the results?
7. What event at the barn dance made an impression on Johnny?

Chapter VI Salt Water Tea

1. What was the grievance the colonists had with England in the Fall of 1773?
2. What was Sam Adams's plan?
3. How had Johnny's feelings about Cilla changed?
4. What did Dr. Warren ask Johnny, and what was his reply?
5. What was the significance of December 16, 1773?
6. What plan was developed in the attic at the *Boston Observer*? Who was the spokesman and one of the creators of the plan?
7. What was Johnny's problem with regard to the plan? What was Rab's suggestion?
8. Describe the events on the night of December 16.

Chapter VII The Fiddler's Bill

1. What punishment did England impose on Boston? What were the effects?
2. What new job did Johnny get? What were the benefits?
3. What news did Johnny hear from Cilla, and how did it affect him?
4. Why did Johnny and Rab put up with Dove?
5. What did Johnny discover when he went to the Lyte house to visit Cilla?

Study Questions *Johnny Tremain* Page 3

Chapter VIII A World to Come

1. What did Johnny discover when he helped Cilla get the Lyte's silver?
2. Describe the encounter between Johnny and Cilla.
3. What event had the Boston Observer Club members upset? What did they do in response?

IX The Scarlet Deluge

1. Describe the spy system.
2. Who were the leaders of the Boston Whigs?
3. What was Johnny's duty?
4. What information did Johnny get from Lydia? What happened as a result of his passing on the information?
5. Describe the relationship between Johnny and Lieutenant Stranger.
6. How did Johnny and Pumpkin help each other?
7. What happened to Pumpkin? What was Johnny's reaction?

Chapter X 'Disperse, Ye Rebels'

1. What information did Johnny find out at the Afric Queen while helping Dove?
2. What was the plan to warn the men in Lexington and Concord?
3. What was the date and location of the first shot fired?
4. What was Johnny doing while the first shot was being fired?

Chapter XI Yankee Doodle

1. Who won at Lexington, and why?
2. Describe the feeling and scene in Boston.
3. What did Johnny want to do, and what did Dr. Warren ask him to do? What did Johnny finally do?
4. What did Lavinia Lyte tell Johnny about his background before she left for England?

XII A Man Can Stand Up

1. What was Johnny's observation as he watched the boats full of wounded British privates and officers being unloaded?
2. How did Johnny get to Charlestown?
3. Describe Johnny's meting with Rab.
4. What did Dr. Warren offer to do for Johnny, and what was Johnny's reply?
5. How did the story end?

ANSWER KEY: SHORT ANSWER STUDY QUESTIONS *Johnny Tremain*

Chapter I Up and About

1. What is the setting of the novel?
   The novel is set in Boston, Massachusetts, in the years 1774-1775.

2. What is Johnny's job?
   He is an apprentice silversmith to Mr. Lapham.

3. How does Johnny get along with Dove and Dusty, and how do they feel about him?
   Johnny bosses them around. Dove fights back, but Dusty is afraid of Johnny.

4. Why did Mr. Lapham have Johnny read the Bible verses?
   He wanted to remind Johnny to be more humble.

5. Which rich merchant came to the shop and why?
   John Hancock came to have a sugar basin made as a present for his aunt. Mr. Lapham had made the original sugar basin that had been damaged.

6. What did Johnny tell Cilla about his middle name and his childhood?
   He told her his middle name was Lyte. His mother was kin to Jonathan Lyte. She gave him the silver cup with the L monogram when she died, and told him to go to Mr. Lyte if he "got to the end of everything."

Chapter II The Pride of Your Power

1. To whom did Johnny go for help with the sugar basin? What was the result?
   He went to Paul Revere, master silversmith. Paul Revere showed him how to make the handles correctly. Then he offered to buy Johnny's unexpired apprentice time from Mr. Lapham.

2. What problem did Johnny encounter with completing the sugar basin? What did he do about it?
   He couldn't complete it on time. He finished making the wax model for the handles on Saturday morning. Dove took a long time going for charcoal. He returned with a very poor quality charcoal, pretending he didn't know it was inferior. Mr. Lapham told Johnny he could not work on Saturday evening. Johnny convinced Mrs. Lapham to let him work on Sunday, which was against the law.

3. Describe Johnny's accident, including who was responsible for it, and what the result was.
   Dove gave Johnny a cracked crucible for melting the silver. As Johnny was reaching out to get the silver he slipped in beeswax that was on the floor. His right hand came down on top of the furnace, and was severely burned. He was ill for several days. Mrs. Lapham treated him as best she could, but when he recovered he found that the thumb and palm had drawn together, and the hand was useless.

4. Describe Mrs. Lapham's treatment of Johnny after the accident.
   At first she tried to humor him. Then she began to call him names. She encouraged Mr. Lapham to tell Johnny to find other work.

5. What did Mr. Lapham tell Johnny after the accident?
   He told Johnny about Dove's part in it. He also said he would keep Johnny at the house, but he had to find a new way to support himself.

Chapter III An Earth of Brass

1. Describe Johnny's method of looking for work. Was it effective?
   He went to the far ends of Boston. He barged into the shops without bothering to look at the type of work being done there. Most of the shopkeepers said they couldn't use him when they saw his hand. One butcher offered him a job, but Johnny didn't want to slaughter animals.

2. Who was Percival Tweedie and why was he important?
   Percival Tweedie was a silversmith from Baltimore. Mrs. Lapham wanted him to take over the business from her father and marry either Madge or Dorcas.

3. Describe Johnny's first encounter with Rab.
   Rab's uncle owned the *Boston Observer*. Johnny met Rab when he went to the *Boston Observer* looking for work. Rab offered Johnny lunch, listened to him talk, and offered him a job. Johnny declined, but said he would come to visit.

4. How did Johnny's looks and dress change after the accident?
   He wore his hat at a rakish angle. He kept his injured hand in his pocket, which made him look arrogant. He sometimes looked shabby and desperate.

5. Describe Isannah's reaction when Johnny tried to pick her up in his arms. How did Johnny feel about it?

She was giggling at first. Then she saw his hand and started screaming not to touch her with the dreadful hand. Johnny was sure that all of the others felt the same way but had not said so. He left the Lapham house and went walking around Boston. He went to the graveyard, flung himself down on his mother's grave, and cried. Then he decided to go to Mr. Lyte.

Chapter IV The Rising Eye

1. What did Mr. Jonathan Lyte think of Johnny's story at first? What did he do after Johnny described the cup?

    At first Mr. Lyte said it was an old story, and others had used it to try and get money out of him. After Johnny described the cup, Mr. Lyte told him to come to his house that evening and bring the cup.

2. Describe Johnny's visit to the Lyte mansion.

    Twelve people from the family were gathered in the drawing room. They went into the dining room to look at the three silver cups on the sideboard. Johnny gave his cup to Mr. Lyte, who compared it to one of his own. Then he accused Johnny of having stolen the cup. He ordered the sheriff, who was also there, to arrest Johnny.

3. How did Rab help Johnny while he was in jail?

    He got Johnny a better cell and a free lawyer named Josiah Quincy. He met with Cilla to make a plan for her to testify in Johnny's behalf.

4. Why was Cilla's testimony important?

    She was the only one who knew Johnny's story, and she had heard it before he went to Mr. Lyte. Her testimony could prove his innocence.

5. Describe the main events and outcome of the trial.

    Mr. Lyte told his version, insisting that Johnny was a thief and should get the death penalty. Then Mr. Quincy had Johnny tell his story. After that, he put Cilla on the stand. She confirmed Johnny's story. As she was finishing, Isannah ran into the courtroom, flung herself at the Justice, and gave her account of the Johnny's story. The Justice dismissed the case, saying there was no evidence that Johnny had stolen the cup, or that Johnny's cup was the one that had been stolen. He gave the one cup back to Johnny. Isannah kissed Johnny's burned hand while they were standing on the sidewalk outside of the courthouse.

Chapter V *The Boston Observer*

1. How did Rab get Cilla to court?
    He showed Mrs. Lapham a letter signed by the governor and stamped with the great seal. He knew she could not read, and he merely said "Governor's orders" and took Cilla. He didn't tell Mrs. Lapham the letter was really addressed to Mr. Lorne.

2. What did Johnny do with his cup, and what was the result?
    He tried to sell it to Mr. Lyte. Mr. Lyte took the cup, again accused Johnny of lying and stealing, and threatened to have him shipped off to Guadalupe with a Captain Bull. Johnny escaped from Mr. Lyte's office, but Mr. Lyte kept the cup.

3. What job did Johnny take?
    He became the horse boy for the Boston Observer. He delivered papers in and around Boston.

4. How did Johnny feel about his job?
    It was a delight. He learned about country life and politics. He enjoyed making grand entrances on his horse.

5. What were the chairs in the attic at the Boston Observer used for?
    "The Boston Observer Club" met at the newspaper office. The men who met there talked of treasonous topics.

6. How did Johnny, under Rab's guidance, begin to change, and what were the results?
    He began spending his time reading, learning to write with his left hand, and exercising his horse. Rab talked to him about his rude manners and Johnny began to watch himself. He discovered that politeness had rewards. Whenever he went to Mr. Adams's house he was invited in, and Mr. Adams began to employ him to do express riding for the Boston Committee of Correspondence.

7. What event at the barn dance made an impression on Johnny?
    Johnny forgot all about his injured hand. The girls danced with him and didn't notice his hand.

Chapter VI Salt Water Tea

1. What was the grievance the colonists had with England in the Fall of 1773?
    There was a tax on tea. The colonists insisted they would not be taxed if they could not vote for the men who taxed them.

2. What was Sam Adams's plan?
    He wanted to prevent the tea from landing at the dock in Boston. He wanted to make sure the tax was not paid. He was calling a meeting of the Observers to plan their strategy.

3. How had Johnny's feelings about Cilla changed?
    He thought he had changed but she had not. He couldn't tell her about his new, secret life, and was not interested in her news. He had an undisclosed romantic attachment to Lavinia Lyte, not Cilla.

4. What did Dr. Warren ask Johnny, and what was his reply?
    Dr. Warren asked Johnny to let him look at the injured hand. Johnny refused. The doctor asked if the injury was God's will? Johnny replied that it was.

5. What was the significance of December 16, 1773?
    That was the day the tea had to be either destroyed or returned to England.

6. What plan was developed in the attic at the *Boston Observer*? Who was the spokesman and one of the creators of the plan?
    Sam Adams told the others about the plan. Rab and Paul Revere would find about thirty young men and boys to throw the tea on the ships overboard into Boston Harbor. They were to dress like Indians so they would not be recognized.

7. What was Johnny's problem with regard to the plan? What was Rab's suggestion?
    He wanted to help but could not use a hatchet to chop open the tea chests. Rab suggested Johnny start to practice by splitting the logs in the back yard.

8. Describe the events on the night of December 16.
    The disguised boys, and Paul Revere, boarded the ships. They chopped open the wooden tea chests, then opened the canvas bags and dumped the tea into the harbor. They didn't damage any of the other cargo. After the tea had all been dumped, they cleaned the decks of the ships. Many people stood on the shore watching. When the last of the tea had been dumped, they all shouted a hurrah. The British Admiral Montague shouted from a window that they would all have to pay the fiddler.

Chapter VII The Fiddler's Bill

1. What punishment did England impose on Boston? What were the effects?
    The rulers in London voted to close the port of Boston. No ships would be allowed in or out. This caused loss of jobs. No food could get in by sea, but the other colonies sent food by wagon. The number of British troops in Boston increased

2. What new job did Johnny get? What were the benefits?
    He began carrying messages for the British troops. He got information about their plans. He also made a lot of money, because he charged them high fees. He made enough to feed the Lorne family.

3. What news did Johnny hear from Cilla, and how did it affect him?
    Cilla told him that Mr. Tweedie wanted to marry her, not Madge. Dorcas ran off with Frizel, Junior. Cilla and Isannah were living with Lavinia Lyte. Johnny felt confused because Cilla had changed so much. He asked if he could see her when he delivered the paper to the Lyte home. Cilla told him to ask the cook about it when he came. Then Johnny got mad when Rab walked Cilla home.

4. Why did Johnny and Rab put up with Dove?
    They thought he might be able to give them valuable information from the British army.

5. What did Johnny discover when he went to the Lyte house to visit Cilla?
    He found out that the cook, Bessie, called herself a "Daughter of Liberty." Cilla and Isannah were treated much differently: Cilla was more of a lady-in-waiting, while Isannah was pampered by Lavinia.

Chapter VIII A World to Come

1. What did Johnny discover when he helped Cilla get the Lyte's silver?
    He found the family Bible, and saw that his mother's name had been scratched out of the genealogy pages. He was able to read the information by holding the book up to a lantern. According to the information in the Bible, she had married Dr. Charles Latour, and both had died in Marseilles, France. Johnny really was the grandnephew of Mr. Lyte. He was puzzled about the inaccurate information in the book.

2. Describe the encounter between Johnny and Cilla.

She mentioned that Rab had been taking her walking and buying her sweets. Johnny was annoyed. Cilla talked about men's last names that would sound right with hers. She said Rab's name, Silsbee, didn't sound good with Priscilla, but Priscilla Tremain sounded fine. Johnny realized he was attracted to her.

3. What event had the Boston Observer Club members upset? What did they do in response?
General Gage had taken the cannon and gunpowder from Charlestown and the Minute Men had not even known about it until it was too late. The club members set up a spy network to make sure they knew what the British were doing.

IX The Scarlet Deluge

1. Describe the spy system.
Paul Revere organized it. 30 of the master artisans were at the center. They constructed a web of workmen, apprentices, and friends who passed on any news they heard.

2. Who were the leaders of the Boston Whigs?
Sam Adams, John Hancock, Dr. Church, and Dr. Warren were the leaders.

3. What was Johnny's duty?
He was to keep track of Colonel Smith and the 10th Regiment, and also be friendly enough with Dove to get information from him.

4. What information did Johnny get from Lydia? What happened as a result of his passing on the information?
The British were planning to take Portsmouth. Paul Revere warned the men and they seized the British stores instead.

5. Describe the relationship between Johnny and Lieutenant Stranger.
They were equals when riding, and Johnny worshipped him. Stranger enjoyed having a worthwhile student. Once indoors, Stranger was a gentleman and a British officer and Johnny was his inferior.

6. How did Johnny and Pumpkin help each other?
Pumpkin saved Johnny from a whipping by telling him to use his spurs on the horse. Johnny got Pumpkin a disguise so he could get out of the militia. In return, Pumpkin gave Johnny his musket. Johnny gave the musket to Rab.

7. What happened to Pumpkin? What was Johnny's reaction?

Pumpkin was shot to death by a British firing squad. Johnny accidentally witnessed the execution, and it unnerved him.

Chapter X 'Disperse, Ye Rebels'

1. What information did Johnny find out at the Afric Queen while helping Dove?
   There was news of a campaign by sea to Lexington and Concord. Colonel Smith was to be in command.

2. What was the plan to warn the men in Lexington and Concord?
   Bentley and Richardson rowed Paul Revere across the river to Charlestown. Then Paul Revere rode to Lexington and Concord. Meanwhile, Robert Newman hung two lanterns in the tower at Christ Church. Billy Dawes got out through the gates of the city by pretending to be a drunkard selling a horse.

3. What was the date and location of the first shot fired?
   It was in Lexington, Massachusetts, on April 19, 1775.

4. What was Johnny doing while the first shot was being fired?
   He was sleeping in Dr. Warren's house.

Chapter XI Yankee Doodle

1. Who won at Lexington, and why?
   The British won because they had 700 well-armed troops and the rebels had only 70 untrained men with inferior weapons.

2. Describe the feeling and scene in Boston.
   The British troops were restless. The local people were wondering what was going on because so many Marines and other troops were moving in and out. General Gage sent for Hancock and the others, but they had already left Boston. There was a general feeling of tension and excitement.

3. What did Johnny want to do, and what did Dr. Warren ask him to do? What did Johnny finally do?
   Johnny wanted to go to the fighting with Dr. Warren. Dr. Warren asked him to stay in Boston and find out as much information as he could. Johnny did as Dr. Warren asked.

4. What did Lavinia Lyte tell Johnny about his background before she left for England?
   She told him that Mr. Lyte truly believed Johnny was an impostor, as one of his cups had been stolen and a young boy was used to pretend to be a relative. Johnny's mother was Vinnie Lyte. She married a naval surgeon and prisoner of war named Dr. Charles Latour. The family was against the marriage because he was a French Catholic. They went to France, where he died. Latour's family sent Vinnie to a convent, where Johnny was born. When Lavinia saw Johnny she did some investigating and found out the whole story. Lavinia told Johnny he could call her Aunt Lavinia.

XII A Man Can Stand Up

1. What was Johnny's observation as he watched the boats full of wounded British privates and officers being unloaded?
   He noticed that the boats with officers had only a few on board, and they were unloaded first. The boats with the privates on them were crowded and were left until last. The wounded privates were not treated well. Johnny thought it was not right to mistreat a man because he was of a lower rank.

2. How did Johnny get to Charlestown?
   He wore Pumpkin's old uniform and said he had a message for Earl Percy.

3. Describe Johnny's meting with Rab. What happened to Rab?
   Rab was in Buckman's Tavern. While Johnny was is the room, Rab pretended to be better than he really was. Rab gave his musket to Johnny and asked him to go to Silsbee's cove to check on his family. Rab died from his wounds and loss of blood.

4. What did Dr. Warren offer to do for Johnny, and what was Johnny's reply?
   Dr. Warren offered to cut through the scar tissue so Johnny could use his injured hand to hold a musket. Johnny accepted the offer.

5. How did the story end?
   Johnny went outside of the tavern to get fresh air while the doctor was getting his instruments ready. He heard the distant sound of "Yankee Doodle." He saw a line of men marching, and behind them was Rab's grandfather. Johnny started to run after him to tell him of Rab's death, but stopped himself.

MULTIPLE CHOICE STUDY QUESTIONS *Johnny Tremain*

Chapter I Up and About

1. What is the setting of the novel?
    A. The novel is set in Philadelphia, Pennsylvania, in 1776.
    B. The novel is set in Washington, DC., in 1864-1866.
    C. The novel is set in Boston, Massachusetts, in 1773-1775.
    D. The novel is set in San Francisco, California, in 1890.

2. What was Johnny's job?
    A. He was an apprentice silversmith to Mr. Lapham.
    B. He was a printer's helper for Ben Franklin.
    C. He was a soldier in the British Army.
    D. He was a clerk in John Hancock's office.

3. How did Johnny get along with Dove and Dusty, and how did they feel about him?
    A. They all got along well. Johnny treated them like his younger brothers.
    B. Johnny and Dusty were friends, but they both picked on Dove.
    C. Dove and Dusty liked Johnny, but he was too shy to be friends with them.
    D. Johnny bossed them around. Dove fought back, but Dusty was afraid of Johnny.

4. Why did Mr. Lapham have Johnny read the Bible verses?
    A. He wanted Johnny to teach the others to read.
    B. He wanted to remind Johnny to be more humble.
    C. His sight was too poor for him to read it himself.
    D. Johnny was his favorite apprentice.

5. Which rich merchant came to the shop and why?
    A. Paul Revere came to borrow one of the boys for a big job.
    B. Sam Adams came to have a special belt buckle made.
    C. John Hancock came to have a sugar basin made as a present for his aunt.
    D. Jothan Lyte came to have his cups engraved with his monogram.

6. True or False: Johnny told Cilla his middle name was Lyte. His mother was related to Jonathan Lyte. She gave him the silver cup with the L monogram when she died, and told him to go to Mr. Lyte if he "got to the end of everything."
    A. True
    B. False

Multiple Choice Questions *Johnny Tremain*
Chapter II The Pride of Your Power

1. True or False: Paul Revere charged Johnny for his advice about the sugar basin.
    A. True
    B. False

2. What did Johnny do when he thought he could not finish the sugar basin on time?
    A. He went to Mr. Hancock and asked for more time.
    B. He bought a similar sugar basin from Paul Revere and gave it to Mr. Hancock.
    C. he made Dove and Dusty work faster to try and finish.
    D. He convinced Mrs. Lapham to let him work on Sunday, which was against the law.

3. Which of the following statements does **not** describe Johnny's accident?
    A. Dusty gave Johnny a cracked crucible for melting the silver.
    B. As Johnny was reaching out to get the silver he slipped in beeswax that was on the floor.
    C. His right hand came down on top of the furnace, and was severely burned.
    D. When he recovered he found that the thumb and palm had drawn together, and the hand was useless.

4. Describe Mrs. Lapham's treatment of Johnny after the accident.
    A. She felt guilty for letting him work on Sunday, so she pampered him.
    B. She couldn't stand the sight of his hand, and made Madge tend to him.
    C. At first she tried to humor him. Then she began to call him names.
    D. She didn't like having him around and made him leave.

5. What did Mr. Lapham tell Johnny after the accident?
    A. He said there was no room in his house for a sinner. He told Johnny to find another place to live.
    B. He told Johnny about Dove's part in it. He also said he would keep Johnny at the house, but he had to find a new way to support himself.
    C. He said Johnny could stay and do chores for six months, but then he had to leave.
    D. He asked Johnny to continue working as best he could, and practice using the injured hand.

Multiple Choice Questions *Johnny Tremain*
Chapter III An Earth of Brass

1. True or False: Johnny's method of looking for work was not effective. He barged into places without bothering to see what the work was.
    A. True
    B. False

2. Who was Percival Tweedie and why was he important?
    A. Percival Tweedie was Mr. Lapham's distant cousin. He was coming to buy the shop from Mr. Lapham.
    B. Percival Tweedie was the new preacher in Boston. Mrs. Lapham was hoping he would be interested in one of her girls.
    C. Percival Tweedie was really an undercover spy for the British. He was pretending to be interested in Mr. Lapham's business so he could find out information about the rebels.
    D. Percival Tweedie was a silversmith from Baltimore. Mrs. Lapham wanted him to take over the business from her father and marry either Madge or Dorcas.

3. Describe Johnny's first encounter with Rab.
    A. They had a fist fight at the wharf.
    B. Rab offered Johnny lunch, listened to him talk, and offered him a job.
    C. Johnny asked Rab for a job but Rab said he didn't have one.
    D. Rab felt sorry for Johnny because he was crippled and gave him some money.

4. Which of the following does **not** describe Johnny's looks after the accident?
    A. He wore his hat at a rakish angle.
    B. He kept his injured hand in his pocket, which made him look arrogant.
    C. His clothes were hanging off of him because he was so thin from not eating.
    D. He sometimes looked shabby and desperate.

5. What was the final event that convinced Johnny to go to Mr. Lyte for help?
    A. His shoes and clothes wore out and he had no money for new ones.
    B. Mrs. Lapham put him out of the house for good and he had nowhere to go.
    C. Isannah screamed at him not to touch her with the dreadful hand.
    D. He had a dream and his mother told him to see Mr. Lyte.

Multiple Choice Questions *Johnny Tremain*
Chapter IV The Rising Eye

1. What did Mr. Jonathan Lyte do after Johnny described the cup?
    A. Mr. Lyte called him a liar and threw him out.
    B. Mr. Lyte examined the cup and said it was a fake.
    C. Mr. Lyte told him to come to his house that evening and bring the cup.
    D. Mr. Lyte laughed and said Johnny was clever but the trick wouldn't work.

2. Which of the following events did **not** happen during Johnny's visit to the Lyte mansion?
    A. Lavinia commented that he looked like a Lyte.
    B. The family went into the dining room to look at the silver cups on the sideboard.
    C. Johnny gave his cup to Mr. Lyte, who compared it to one of his own.
    D. Mr. Lyte ordered the sheriff to arrest Johnny for stealing the cup.

3. Who helped Johnny while he was in jail?
    A. Mr. Lorne did.
    B. Rab did.
    C. John Hancock did
    D. Mr. Lapham did.

4. Whose testimony could prove Johnny's innocence? This person was the only one who knew Johnny's story, and had heard it before he went to Mr. Lyte.
    A. Mr. Lapham
    B. Rab
    C. Isannah
    D. Cilla

5. Which of the following did **not** happen at the trial?
    A. Mr. Lyte asked for leniency for Johnny, and said he only wanted his cup back.
    B. Cilla took the stand and confirmed Johnny's story.
    C. The Justice said there was no evidence that Johnny had stolen the cup.
    D. Isannah kissed Johnny's burned had outside the courthouse.

Multiple Choice Questions *Johnny Tremain*
Chapter V *The Boston Observer*

1. How did Rab get Cilla to court?
    A. He paid Mrs. Lapham two silver dollars.
    B. He promised Cilla bag of sweets if she came with him.
    C. He dressed as a guard and said she was under arrest for helping Johnny.
    D. He showed Mrs. Lapham a letter signed and sealed by the governor.

2. What did Johnny do with his cup?
    A. He tried to sell it to Mr. Lyte.
    B. He gave it to Cilla for safekeeping.
    C. He asked Paul Revere to melt it down and give him the money for it.
    D. He put it back in his trunk and forgot about it.

3. What job did Johnny take?
    A. He became a waiter at the Afric Queen.
    B. He delivered papers for the *Boston Observer*.
    C. He began studying law with Josiah Quincy.
    D. He became the town crier.

4. True or False: Johnny disliked his new job and wished he could be a silversmith again.
    A. True
    B. False

5. What were the chairs in the attic at the *Boston Observer* used for?
    A. The shop was used for church on Sundays.
    B. Mr. Lorne rented them to people having large parties, and to the British soldiers when they had meetings.
    C. Mr. Lorne had a second business as a carpenter. He was making them to send to the Constitutional Convention in Philadelphia.
    D. "The Boston Observer Club" met at the newspaper office. The men who met there talked of treasonous topics.

6. Which was **not** one of the changes in Johnny under Rab's guidance?
    A. He began spending his time reading and learning to write with his left hand.
    B. He became less shy with girls and began courting.
    C. He became more polite.
    D. He began to do express riding for the Boston Committee of Correspondence.

Multiple Choice Questions *Johnny Tremain*
Chapter V Continued

7. What event at the barn dance made an impression on Johnny?
   A. Johnny forgot all about his injured hand. The girls danced with him and didn't notice his hand.
   B. Johnny didn't realize he could dance as well as he could.
   C. Johnny saw Cilla dancing with a British officer and got jealous.
   D. Johnny discovered he had an ear for music, and was able to play a tune on the fiddle.

Multiple Choice Questions *Johnny Tremain*
Chapter VI Salt Water Tea

1. What was the grievance the colonists had with England in the Fall of 1773?
    A. There was a tax on tea. The colonists insisted they would not be taxed if they could not vote for the men who taxed them.
    B. The people were not allowed to worship as they pleased. They all had to belong to the Church of England.
    C. All mail in and out of Boston was inspected by the British soldiers. The colonist said this was an invasion of their privacy.
    D. All boys over the age of thirteen had to go to England to serve in the Army. The townspeople didn't want their young men to go.

2. Who is being described? He wanted to prevent the tea from landing at the dock in Boston. He wanted to make sure the tax was not paid. He was calling a meeting of the Observers to plan their strategy.
    A. Paul Revere
    B. John Hancock
    C. Sam Adams
    D. James Otis

3. How had Johnny's feelings about Cilla changed?
    A. He thought they had grown closer.
    B. He thought she had matured too much for him. He wasn't ready for a romance.
    C. He was angry because she insulted him every time she saw him.
    D. He thought he had changed but she had not.

4. True or False: Johnny asked Dr. Warren to look at his hand, but Dr. Warren refused.
    A. True
    B. False

5. What was the significance of December 16, 1773?
    A. The first shot of the war was fired.
    B. The British soldiers took over Boston.
    C. It was Johnny's sixteenth birthday.
    D. That was the day the tea had to be either destroyed or returned to England.

Multiple Choice Questions *Johnny Tremain*
Chapter VI Continued

6. What plan was developed in the attic at the *Boston Observer*?
    A. The tea would be stolen and given to the citizens.
    B. The tea would be burned, along with the ships.
    C. The tea on the ships was to be thrown overboard into Boston Harbor.
    D. The ships would be moved to the ocean and sunk.

7. True or False: Johnny practiced for the event by splitting the logs in the back yard.
    A. True
    B. False

8. Which of the following did **not** happen on the night of December 16?
    A. The men and boys disguised themselves as Indians.
    B. They damaged all of the cargo on the ships, not just the tea.
    C. Many people stood on the shore watching.
    D. Admiral Montague shouted from a window that they would all have to pay the fiddler.

Multiple Choice Questions *Johnny Tremain*
Chapter VII The Fiddler's Bill

1. What punishment did England impose on Boston?
    A. Every man had to do a year of service in the British army.
    B. Two British soldiers moved into each house in and around Boston.
    C. All of the leading citizens were arrested and put in jail.
    D. The port of Boston was closed. People lost jobs and began to starve.

2. What new job did Johnny get? What were the benefits?
    A. He became assistant printer for Mr. Lorne. He became well-informed.
    B. He became Dr. Warren's assistant. He enjoyed helping the sick, and was paid with food and clothes.
    C. He began carrying messages for the British troops. He got information about their plans. He also made a lot of money, because he charged them high fees.
    D. He became Paul Revere's apprentice and was able to learn to use his crippled hand to make silver.

3. Which of the following statements was **not** part of the news Johnny heard from Cilla?
    A. Mr. Tweedie wanted to marry Cilla.
    B. Dorcas ran off with Frizel, Junior.
    C. Mr. Lapham had died, and Tweedie had taken over the business.
    D. Cilla and Isannah were living with Lavinia Lyte.

4. Why did Johnny and Rab put up with Dove?
    A. He might be able to give them valuable information from the British army.
    B. Johnny was still plotting he revenge for Dove's part in his accident.
    C. Mr. Lorne said they had to be kind to everyone.
    D. Dove had a lot of money and treated them to food and entertainment.

5. What did Johnny discover when he went to the Lyte house to visit Cilla?
    A. Cilla was treated more as a servant than a guest.
    B. The cook was a Tory spy.
    C. Isannah had become homesick, but Lavinia wouldn't let her go home.
    D. Both of the girls were going to be sent to boarding school in England.

Multiple Choice Questions *Johnny Tremain*
Chapter VIII A World to Come

1. What did Johnny discover when he helped Cilla get the Lyte's silver?
    A. He found the missing two silver cups.
    B. He found his birth certificate, and a packet of letters from his mother to Mr. Lyte's wife.
    C. He found the family Bible, and saw that his mother's name had been scratched out of the genealogy pages.
    D. He discovered that all of the silver had originally belonged to his mother. Mr. Lyte had stolen it from her before she left the country with her new husband.

2. What did Johnny realize during his encounter with Cilla?
    A. He realized she was better off with Rab, and told her so.
    B. Johnny realized he was attracted to her.
    C. He realized he really loved Lavinia Lyte.
    D. Johnny realized he was more interested in fighting for the cause than in romance.

3. What event got the Boston Observer Club members upset?
    A. General Gage had taken the cannon and gunpowder from Charlestown and the Minute Men had not even known about it until it was too late.
    B. The British had set up a spy ring all around Boston.
    C. The British had barricaded the roads leading into and out of Boston, so no food or supplies could get through.
    D. Many people in Boston were saying they wanted to pay the tea tax and get on with their lives. They were tired of resisting the British.

Multiple Choice Questions *Johnny Tremain*
IX The Scarlet Deluge

1. Which of the following does **not** describe the spy system?
    A. 30 of the master artisans were at the center.
    B. John Hancock organized it.
    C. Workers, friends, and apprentices passed on all news about the British.
    D. The leaders met at the Green Dragon.

2. True or False: Sam Adams, John Hancock, Dr. Church, and Dr. Warren were the leaders of the Boston Whigs.
    A. True
    B. False

3. What was Johnny's duty?
    A. He was to damage the British soldiers' riding gear so that they would be injured when they went riding.
    B. He was to keep track of Colonel Smith and the 10th Regiment, and also be friendly enough with Dove to get information from him.
    C. He was to deliver papers and take secret messages to the members of the club.
    D. He was to keep a journal with all of the information sent in by members of the spy ring.

4. What happened because Johnny passed on the information from Lydia?
    A. John Hancock avoided being arrested.
    B. The Minute Men captured a whole regiment of British soldiers.
    C. Paul Revere warned the men in Portsmouth and they seized the British stores.
    D. The Revolutionary War began.

5. Whose relationship is being described here? They were equals when riding, and Johnny worshipped him. He enjoyed having a worthwhile student. Once indoors, he was a gentleman and an officer and Johnny was his inferior.
    A. Johnny and Earl Percy
    B. Johnny and Colonel Smith
    C. Johnny and General Gage
    D. Johnny and Lieutenant Stranger

Multiple Choice Questions *Johnny Tremain*
Chapter IX Continued

6. What did Pumpkin give Johnny in return for the disguise?
    A. Pumpkin gave Johnny a detailed map of the next British campaign.
    B. Pumpkin gave Johnny his military uniform.
    C. Pumpkin gave Johnny his musket. Johnny gave the musket to Rab.
    D. Pumpkin gave Johnny five British shillings and a one pound note.

7. True or False: Pumpkin was shot to death by a British firing squad.
    A. True
    B. False

Multiple Choice Questions *Johnny Tremain*
Chapter X 'Disperse, Ye Rebels'

1. What information did Johnny find out at the Afric Queen while helping Dove?
    A. Colonel Smith was to go to Lexington and Concord by sea.
    B. General Gage was going to Middlesex and Dartmouth by land.
    C. Lieutenant Stranger was going to Concord and Portsmouth by sea.
    D. General Court was going to Lexington and Marblehead by sea.

2. Which of the following was **not** part of the plan to warn the men in the towns that were going to be attacked?
    A. Bentley and Richardson rowed Paul Revere across the river to Charlestown.
    B. Paul Revere rode to Lexington and Concord.
    C. Robert Newman hung two lanterns in the tower at Christ Church.
    D. Billy Dawes got out through the city gates by pretending to be an old woman.

3. What was the date and location of the first shot fired?
    A. It was in Concord, Massachusetts, on May 21, 1776.
    B. It was in Lexington, Massachusetts, on April 19, 1775.
    C. It was in Boston, Massachusetts, on July 4, 1776.
    D. It was in Charlestown, Massachusetts, on December 16, 1774.

4. What was Johnny doing while the first shot was being fired?
    A. He was writing an article for the paper.
    B. He was marching with the militia.
    C. He was sleeping in Dr. Warren's house.
    D. He was taking a fresh horse and food to Paul Revere.

Multiple Choice Questions *Johnny Tremain*
Chapter XI Yankee Doodle

1. True or False: The rebels won at Lexington because they fought more fiercely.
    A. True
    B. False

2. Describe the feeling and scene in Boston.
    A. The citizens were terrified and wanted to surrender.
    B. Most people on both sides were in a state of shock and disbelief.
    C. Panic had set in and there was confusion and an uproar.
    D. There was a general feeling of tension and excitement.

3. What did Johnny do when Dr. Warren went to find the troops?
    A. He went to join the Minute Men.
    B. He delivered as many of the newspapers as he could.
    C. He stayed in Boston and find out as much information as he could.
    D. He went to the Lyte house to make sure Cilla was safe.

4. Which of the following statements was **not** part of what Lavinia Lyte told Johnny?
    A. Mr. Lyte knew Johnny was telling the truth, but didn't want to admit it.
    B. Johnny's mother was Vinnie Lyte. She married Dr. Charles Latour.
    C. Johnny's father died in France.
    D. Vinnie's maid arranged for her and Johnny to return to America.

Multiple Choice Questions *Johnny Tremain*
<u>XII A Man Can Stand Up</u>

1. What was Johnny's observation as he watched the boats full of wounded British soldiers being unloaded?
    A. He thought the bloodshed was a terrible waste of lives on both sides.
    B. The wounded officers and privates were treated differently. He thought this was unfair.
    C. He was glad there were so many wounded. He hoped they would leave Boston soon.
    D. He was disappointed that he had not been in the fighting himself.

2. How did Johnny get to Charlestown?
    A. He dressed as a girl and took a few cows out of the city to the pasture. Then he walked.
    B. He swam across the river.
    C. He hid in a British supply wagon.
    D. He wore Pumpkin's old uniform and said he had a message for Earl Percy.

3. What happened to Rab?
    A. He died from the wounds and loss of blood.
    B. He was injured but went back to the fighting.
    C. He went to Silsbee Cove to rest.
    D. He deserted and was never heard from again.

4. True or False: Johnny accepted Dr. Warren's offer to cut through the scar tissue so Johnny could use his injured hand to hold a musket.
    A. True
    B. False

5. How did the story end?
    A. Johnny heard the Minute Men coming. He took Rab's musket and went to join them.
    B. He found Cilla and asked her to marry him before he went off to war. She agreed.
    C. Johnny saw Rab's grandfather. He started to tell him about Rab, but stopped himself.
    D. Johnny went out into the fresh air and started to whistle "Yankee Doodle."

ANSWER KEY-MULTIPLE CHOICE STUDY GUIDE/QUIZ QUESTIONS
Johnny Tremain

Chapter I
1. C
2. A
3. D
4. B
5. C
6. A True

Chapter II
1. B False
2. D
3. A
4. C
5. B

Chapter III
1. A
2. D
3. B
4. C
5. C

Chapter IV
1. C
2. A
3. B
4. D
5. A

Chapter V
1. D
2. A
3. B
4. B False
5. D
6. B
7. A

Chapter VI
1. A
2. C
3. D
4. B False
5. D
6. C
7. A True
8. B

Chapter VII
1. D
2. C
3. C
4. A
5. A

Chapter VIII
1. C
2. B
3. A

Chapter IX
1. D
2. A True
3. B
4. C
5. D
6. C
7. A

Chapter X
1. A
2. D
3. B
4. C

Chapter XI
1. B False
2. D
3. C
4. A

Chapter XII
1. B
2. D
3. A
4. A True
5. C

PREREADING VOCABULARY WORKSHEETS

Vocabulary Worksheet *Johnny Tremain*

Chapter I Up and About
Part I: Using Prior Knowledge and Context Clues
Below are the sentences in which the vocabulary words appear in the text. Read the sentence. Use any clues you can find in the sentence combined with your prior knowledge, and write what you think the underlined words mean on the lines provided.

1. ... Mrs. Lapham stood at the foot of a ladder leading to the attic where her father-in-law's *apprentices* slept.

   _____

2. Whatever a 'pig-of-a-louse' was, it did describe the whitish, *flaccid*, parasitic Dove.

   _____

3. Whatever a 'pig-of-a-louse' was, it did describe the whitish, flaccid, *parasitic* Dove.

   _____

4. She wore her clothes so tight (hoping to look *ethereal*), she looked apoplectic.

   _____

5. She wore her clothes so tight (hoping to look ethereal), she looked *apoplectic*.

   _____

6. 'So get out a *crucible.* Soon as Dusty's got the furnace going, you melt it down and try again.'

   _____

7. 'What is it, my girl?' He often thus *arrogantly* addressed his master's grand-daughters--really his own mistress.

   _____

8. At last Mr. Lapham raised his *protuberant* eyes.

   _____

Vocabulary Worksheet *Johnny Tremain*
Chapter I Up and About

Part II: Determining the Meaning

Match the vocabulary words to their dictionary definitions.

____ 1.	apprentices	A.	lacking in vigor or energy
____ 2.	flaccid	B.	boastfully
____ 3.	parasitic	C.	airy; fragile
____ 4.	ethereal	D.	swelling outward; bulging
____ 5.	apoplectic	E.	unpaid workers who learn a trade or craft
____ 6.	crucible	F.	porcelain dish used for melting silver
____ 7.	arrogantly	G.	taking advantage of others without return
____ 8.	protuberant	H.	loss of muscular control and sensation

Vocabulary Worksheet *Johnny Tremain*

Chapter II The Pride of Your Power
Part I: Using Prior Knowledge and Context Clues
Below are the sentences in which the vocabulary words appear in the text. Read the sentence. Use any clues you can find in the sentence combined with your prior knowledge, and write what you think the underlined words mean on the lines provided.

1. Johnny was so anxious to be on with the work--*tediously* delayed by Dove's tricks--he hardly listened.

    _____

2. 'It's sinful to let yourself go so over *mundane* things.'

    _____

3. Mrs. Lapham had plunged the burned hand into a panful of flour and was yelling at Madge to hurry with her bread *poultice*.

    _____

4. The fever *abated* and with it the doses of the drug.

    _____

5. No one *reproved* him because he had disobeyed Mrs. Lapham.

    _____

6. The old man had never once *berated* him for Sabbath-breaking, never reminded him how often he had pointed out that pride goeth before a fall.

    _____

7. 'I can't help but admit I'm encouraged with that much *piety* in one of my boys.'

    _____

Vocabulary Worksheet *Johnny Tremain*
Chapter II The Pride of Your Power

Part II: Determining the Meaning

Match the vocabulary words to their dictionary definitions.

_____ 1. tediously   A. reduced in amount
_____ 2. mundane   B. found fault with
_____ 3. poultice   C. slowly; in a boring manner
_____ 4. abated   D. rebuked; scolded
_____ 5. reproved   E. reverence
_____ 6. berated   F. dressing for a wound or injury
_____ 7. piety   G. ordinary

Vocabulary Worksheet *Johnny Tremain*

Chapter III An Earth of Brass
Part I: Using Prior Knowledge and Context Clues
Below are the sentences in which the vocabulary words appear in the text. Read the sentence. Use any clues you can find in the sentence combined with your prior knowledge, and write what you think the underlined words mean on the lines provided.

1. He lifted his dark face, *indolent* dark eyes.

    _____

2. He told about the burn, but with none of the *belligerent* arrogance with which he had been answering the questions kind people had put to him.

    _____

3. She was trying to nurse him along, to get the *wary* creature to sign her contract and marry one of her girls.

    _____

4. The lower floor of the Town House was an open *promenade* and here every day the merchants gathered 'on 'change.'

    _____

5. From where he sat on the steps of the Town House, he could look the brief length of King Street which quickly and *imperceptibly* turned into Long Wharf, running for half a mile into the sea.

    _____

6. He had been attracted by the quality of the boy's voice, for, although Johnny often spoke in the rougher, slurring manner of Hancock's Wharf, in reading he *reverted* to the cleaner speech his mother had taught him.

    _____

7. Mr. Hancock quickly *averted* his fine eyes.

    _____

Vocabulary Worksheet *Johnny Tremain*
Chapter III An Earth of Brass

Part II: Determining the Meaning
Match the vocabulary words to their dictionary definitions.

_____ 1. indolent   A. habitually lazy
_____ 2. belligerent   B. on guard; watchful
_____ 3. wary   C. hardly noticed
_____ 4. promenade   D. turned away
_____ 5. imperceptibly   E. eager to fight; hostile
_____ 6. reverted   F. returned to a former condition
_____ 7. averted   G. a public place for walking

Vocabulary Worksheet *Johnny Tremain*

Chapter IV The Rising Eye
Part I: Using Prior Knowledge and Context Clues
Below are the sentences in which the vocabulary words appear in the text. Read the sentence. Use any clues you can find in the sentence combined with your prior knowledge, and write what you think the underlined words mean on the lines provided.

1. Although Johnny might have been more *cordially* received by Merchant Lyte, he was satisfied enough with his welcome to build up air castles.

   _____

2. Johnny's life with the Laphams had been so limited he knew little of the political *strife* which was turning Boston into two armed camps.

   _____

3. The Whigs declaring taxation without representation is *tyranny*.

   _____

4. He had been expecting some such *apparition* from the past ever since last August.

   _____

5. Rab, *enigmatical*, dark, capable, looked as always.

   _____

Part II: Determining the Meaning
Match the vocabulary words to their dictionary definitions.

_____ 1. cordially   A. a ghostly figure
_____ 2. strife   B. graciously; in a friendly manner
_____ 3. tyranny   C. unjust use of absolute power
_____ 4. apparition   D. puzzling
_____ 5. enigmatical   E. a struggle or fight

Vocabulary Worksheet *Johnny Tremain*

Chapter V *The Boston Observer*
Part I: Using Prior Knowledge and Context Clues
Below are the sentences in which the vocabulary words appear in the text. Read the sentence. Use any clues you can find in the sentence combined with your prior knowledge, and write what you think the underlined words mean on the lines provided.

1. It had been sent to Mr. Lorne, commanding him and the other printers of Boston to quit their <u>seditious</u>, rebellious publications--or else.

   _____

2. 'Mr. Hadden and Mr. Barton, you are witnesses of his <u>repentance</u> and voluntary return of my stolen property.'

   _____

3. When people on the streets or at the taverns complimented him on his mount, there would come the same <u>fatuous</u> expression on his face he had often ridiculed on Cilla's when people stopped her and said how angelic Isannah was, but he did not know it.

   _____

4. It was a secret club, as powerful as any in Boston, and here in the last few years had been hatched much '<u>treason</u>' as the Tories called it.

   _____

5. Then she would feel so fond of the lonely boy, who never knew he was lonely, and so amused at his <u>pretense</u> of scorn for something he in his heart loved, she could not help but kiss him.

   _____

6. Johnny thought in amazement how <u>nonchalant</u> and even sluggish Rab could seem about the printing shop, and yet he did his work with a machine-like perfection.

   _____

Vocabulary Worksheet *Johnny Tremain*
Chapter V *The Boston Observer*

Part II: Determining the Meaning
Match the vocabulary words to their dictionary definitions.

____ 1.	seditious	A.	a false action intended to deceive
____ 2.	repentance	B.	unconsciously foolish
____ 3.	fatuous	C.	rebellious
____ 4.	treason	D.	remorse; contrition
____ 5.	pretense	E.	unconcerned; indifferent
____ 6.	nonchalant	F.	betrayal of one's country

Vocabulary Worksheet *Johnny Tremain*

Chapter VI Salt Water Tea
Part I: Using Prior Knowledge and Context Clues
Below are the sentences in which the vocabulary words appear in the text. Read the sentence. Use any clues you can find in the sentence combined with your prior knowledge, and write what you think the underlined words mean on the lines provided.

1. England had, by the fall of 1773, gone far in adjusting the *grievances* of her American colonies.

   _____

2. Mr. Hancock had indeed found a smith to make it after Mr. Lapham failed so *lamentably*.

   _____

3. Johnny went to the door to see what the *clamor* was. A courageous Tory was chasing the men whom he had found tacking a placard on his property.

   _____

4. 'Gentlemen,' he said, 'tonight we have made our decision--and know the method by which the *detested* tea can be destroyed, if the ships are not allowed to return.'

   _____

5. 'The mass meetings which will be held almost daily demanding the return of the tea are to *arouse* public opinion and to persuade the world we did not turn to violence until every other course had been blocked to us.'

   _____

6. 'Not one is to be told in advance just what the work will be, not who the others are, nor the names of the men who *instigated* this tea party--that is, the gentlemen who are here tonight.'

   _____

7. Sometimes Rab and Johnny went to these meetings. It happened they were there when the sheriff arrived and bade the meeting forthwith to *disperse*.

   _____

Vocabulary Worksheet *Johnny Tremain*
Chapter VI Salt Water Tea

8. His teeth looked sharp and white as an animal's. In spite of his calm *demeanor*, calm voice, he was charged and surcharged with a will to action, a readiness to take and enjoy any desperate chance.

_____

Part II: Determining the Meaning
Match the vocabulary words to their dictionary definitions.

_____ 1. grievances   A. uproar
_____ 2. lamentable   B. promoted the growth of; incited
_____ 3. clamor   C. reasons for protest
_____ 4. detested   D. the way in which a person behaves
_____ 5. arouse   E. hated
_____ 6. instigated   F. regrettable
_____ 7. disperse   G. to scatter in different directions
_____ 8. demeanor   H. awaken or excite

Vocabulary Worksheet *Johnny Tremain*

Chapter VII The Fiddler's Bill
Part I: Using Prior Knowledge and Context Clues
Below are the sentences in which the vocabulary words appear in the text. Read the sentence. Use any clues you can find in the sentence combined with your prior knowledge, and write what you think the underlined words mean on the lines provided.

1. But when that bill came--the fiddler's bill--that bill for the tea, it was so much heavier than anyone expected, Boston was thrown into a *paroxysm* of anger and despair.

   _____

2. Boston was *inundated* with British soldiers, and now every third person one met in the street wore the handsome uniform of King George the Third.

   _____

3. He did not stop the flood of treasonable *oratory* which poured forth from men like Warren and Quincy.

   _____

4. True enough, there were boys no older than he drilling there, but his crippled hand made it impossible for him to pull a trigger. This *incapacity* fretted him badly and he would sometimes take it out on Rab.

   _____

5. He got up, ruefully looked at his white breeches, shrugged, and walked over to where Johnny was *diligently* pinning up sheets.

   _____

6. He remembered when there was no money to buy meat and how she would go from stall to stall until she found another who would accept payment by a new clasp on his pocketbook, or a fishwife who would exchange a basket of salt herrings for a black mourning ring. Her *bartering* and bickering had then seemed small-minded to him; now he was enough older to realize how valiantly she had fought for those under her care.

   _____

Vocabulary Worksheet *Johnny Tremain*
Chapter VII The Fiddler's Bill

7. Gale, whose legs must have been badly cramped, picked up Madge as though she were a pet cat and sat her down beside him. The little man must be *prodigiously* strong, thought Johnny, and he liked his ugly, lined face.

_____

8. Her eyes *wavered* and she did not finish her sentence.

_____

Chapter VII The Fiddler's Bill

Part II: Determining the Meaning
Match the vocabulary words to their dictionary definitions.

___ 1.	paroxysm	A.	in a hardworking manner
___ 2.	inundated	B.	public speaking
___ 3.	oratory	C.	impressively great ; enormously
___ 4.	incapacity	D.	a spasm or fit
___ 5.	diligently	E.	trading goods or services without money
___ 6.	bartering	F.	inadequate strength or ability
___ 7.	prodigiously	G.	showed indecision
___ 8.	wavered	H.	overwhelmed; swamped

Vocabulary Worksheet *Johnny Tremain*

Chapter VIII A World to Come
Part I: Using Prior Knowledge and Context Clues
Below are the sentences in which the vocabulary words appear in the text. Read the sentence. Use any clues you can find in the sentence combined with your prior knowledge, and write what you think the underlined words mean on the lines provided.

1. But here were a few *turbulent* fellows hanging about an inn door, and in Milton itself they were signaled to stop by a group whose faces they never did see.
   _____

2. That musket which Rab did not have bothered Johnny. However, the soldiers never carried them while *loitering* about alehouses and wharves, or the stables of the Afric Queen.
   _____

3. 'They won't come back because there is going to be a war--*civil* war. And we'll win.'
   _____

4. Now he was blocked and it made him restless, possibly less *canny*.
   _____

5. It was well enough to say Rab was secretive by nature and couldn't help the way God had made him, but Johnny felt *piqued*.
   _____

6. Ever since he had grown so queer, the other members did not wish him about, even in his *lucid* periods. They talked and talked.
   _____

7. 'For ten years we've tried this and we've tried that. We've tried to *placate* them and they to *placate* us. Gentlemen, you know it has not worked.'
   _____

Vocabulary Worksheet *Johnny Tremain*
Chapter VIII A World to Come

Part II: Determining the Meaning
Match the vocabulary words to their dictionary definitions.

____ 1. turbulent   A. easily understood; intelligible
____ 2. loitering   B. relating to a citizen
____ 3. civil   C. careful and shrewd
____ 4. canny   D. violently agitated or disturbed
____ 5. piqued   E. felt wounded pride
____ 6. lucid   F. to appease; to make concessions
____ 7. placate   G. standing idly about; lingering aimlessly

Vocabulary Worksheet *Johnny Tremain*

Chapter IX The Scarlet Deluge
Part I: Using Prior Knowledge and Context Clues
Below are the sentences in which the vocabulary words appear in the text. Read the sentence. Use any clues you can find in the sentence combined with your prior knowledge, and write what you think the underlined words mean on the lines provided.

1. All such news, important and *trivial*, was carried to the thirty, meeting secretly at the Green Dragon.

   _____

2. As soon as Johnny began to *cultivate* Dove, he was surprised at the response.

   _____

3. He knew Colonel Smith had told Lydia that one of his young gentlemen was prone to *solitary* tippling.

   _____

4. Johnny filled his tankard again with the horrifying *concoction*.

   _____

5. He was an *ardent* teacher who had at last met a pupil worth bothering with.

   _____

6. She made them so large she believed they would last him through his *indenture*.

   _____

7. Had Rab ever felt as he did now? You could not guess by looking at him. If he had any *qualms*, he would never mention them.

   _____

Vocabulary Worksheet *Johnny Tremain*
Chapter IX The Scarlet Deluge

Part II: Determining the Meaning
Match the vocabulary words to their dictionary definitions.

____ 1. trivial   A. passionate; displaying strong enthusiasm
____ 2. cultivate   B. to nurture; to foster
____ 3. solitary   C. uneasy feelings
____ 4. concoction   D. alone
____ 5. ardent   E. of little significance or value
____ 6. indenture   F. unpaid service to another
____ 7. qualms   G. a food or beverage made of mixed ingredients

Vocabulary Worksheet *Johnny Tremain*

Chapter X 'Disperse, Ye Rebels'
Part I: Using Prior Knowledge and Context Clues
Below are the sentences in which the vocabulary words appear in the text. Read the sentence. Use any clues you can find in the sentence combined with your prior knowledge, and write what you think the underlined words mean on the lines provided.

1. Johnny read it on Colonel Smith's face. . . Was it *martial* ardor?

    _____

2. He did not seem to feel any grief at abandoning Johnny, who sat *disconsolately* on his bed watching Rab.

    _____

3. Seemingly Gage, a *punctilious* man, had chosen Francis Smith because he had been in service longer than any of the other (and smarter) colonels.

    _____

4. The young man stuck a *dilapidated* hat with a broken feather on his head and his wife picked up a bottle of rum and poured it over the front of his torn jacket.

    _____

5. But each knew the other was in deadly *peril* of his life.

    _____

Part II: Determining the Meaning
Match the vocabulary words to their dictionary definitions.

____ 1. martial   A. broken down and shabby
____ 2. disconsolately   B. cheerless; gloomy
____ 3. punctilious   C. imminent danger
____ 4. dilapidated   D. relating to war
____ 5. peril   E. precise; scrupulous

Vocabulary Worksheet *Johnny Tremain*

Chapter XI Yankee Doodle
Part I: Using Prior Knowledge and Context Clues
Below are the sentences in which the vocabulary words appear in the text. Read the sentence. Use any clues you can find in the sentence combined with your prior knowledge, and write what you think the underlined words mean on the lines provided.

1. 'I'd rather die fighting than on a gallows. Gage won't be so *lenient* now-- soon as he learns war has begun.'

   _____

2. On Cornhill Johnny could feel the *subdued* excitement. Everyone knew something was happening.

   _____

3. Earl Percy and his *laggard* brigade were gone.

   _____

4. 'They are all going to London until this *insurrection*, as they call it, is over.'

   _____

5. A little *diffidently* Isannah emerged from behind the lady's great dark skirts.

   _____

6. 'Yes, dear, you will --when I am Lady Pryor-Morton and you my little *protégée*.'

   _____

7. 'Then his family, of course, would have none of her, she being a *heretic*.'

   _____

8. He said it *tentatively*. 'Aunt Lavinia?'

   _____

Vocabulary Worksheet *Johnny Tremain*
Chapter XI Yankee Doodle

Part II: Determining the Meaning
Match the vocabulary words to their dictionary definitions.

_____ 1. lenient   A. uncertainly; hesitantly
_____ 2. subdued   B. open revolt against a government
_____ 3. laggard   C. misbeliever
_____ 4. insurrection   D. brought under control; quieted
_____ 5. diffidently   E. a girl whose welfare is promoted by another
_____ 6. protégée   F. hanging back or falling behind
_____ 7. heretic   G. shyly; timidly
_____ 8. tentatively   H. merciful; indulgent

Vocabulary Worksheet *Johnny Tremain*

Chapter XII A Man Can Stand Up
Part I: Using Prior Knowledge and Context Clues
Below are the sentences in which the vocabulary words appear in the text. Read the sentence. Use any clues you can find in the sentence combined with your prior knowledge, and write what you think the underlined words mean on the lines provided.

1. Although no townsmen, except only the doctors, were permitted on the wharf, Johnny knew that hundreds of them stood well back in darkness, *gloating*.

   _____

2. He had seen so much of the British army he had come to believe that they were, even as they said, *invincible*. No Yankee farmers could stand up to them.

   _____

3. The smashed meeting house with its tiny wooden *belfry* was before him.

   _____

4. Tired as he was and *surfeited* with the sight of blood and suffering, he broke the news as best he could.

   _____

5. The doctor looked at him with *compassionate* eyes.

   _____

6. A curious *arsenal* of *weapons*.

   _____

Vocabulary Worksheet *Johnny Tremain*
Chapter XII A Man Can Stand Up

Part II: Determining the Meaning
Match the vocabulary words to their dictionary definitions.

_____ 1. gloating   A. a bell tower
_____ 2. invincible   B. unconquerable
_____ 3. belfry   C. a supply of weapons
_____ 4. surfeited   D. sympathetic
_____ 5. compassionate   E. expressing self-satisfaction
_____ 6. arsenal   F. saturated; over-filled

ANSWER KEY-PREREADING VOCABULARY WORKSHEETS

Chapter I
1. E
2. A
3. G
4. C
5. H
6. F
7. B
8. D

Chapter II
1. C
2. G
3. F
4. A
5. B
6. D
7. E

Chapter III
1. A
2. E
3. B
4. G
5. C
6. F
7. D

Chapter IV
1. B
2. E
3. C
4. A
5. D

Chapter V
1. C
2. D
3. B
4. F
5. A
6. E

Chapter VI
1. C
2. F
3. A
4. E
5. H
6. B
7. G
8. D

Chapter VII
1. D
2. H
3. B
4. F
5. A
6. E
7. C
8. G

Chapter VIII
1. D
2. G
3. B
4. C
5. E
6. A
7. F

Chapter IX
1. E
2. B
3. D
4. G
5. A
6. F
7. C

Chapter X
1. D
2. B
3. E
4. A
5. C

Chapter XI
1. H
2. D
3. F
4. B
5. G
6. E
7. C
8. A

Chapter XII
1. E
2. B
3. A
4. F
5. D
6. C

DAILY LESSONS

LESSON ONE

<u>Objectives</u>
    1. To introduce the *Johnny Tremain* unit
    2. To relate students' prior knowledge to the new material
    3. To distribute books and other related materials (study guides, reading assignments)
    4. To introduce the genre of historical fiction
    5. To do the prereading work for Chapter I

<u>Activity #1</u>
    Decorate a bulletin board with a map of pre-Revolutionary War colonial America. Display some pictures of Boston around 1774. Bring artifacts such as a tricorner hat, loose tea, paper, stamps, a silver sugar bowl, and the flag of England. Play a recording of Yankee Doodle or other colonial era music. Ask students to tell you what they know about the American colonies in the early 1700s, about Boston, the novel, and Esther Forbes. Do a group KWL sheet with the students (form included.) Put any information the students know in the K column (What I Know.) Ask students what they want to find out and put that information in the W column (What I Want to Find Out.) Keep the sheet and refer back to it while reading. After reading the novel, complete the L column (What I Learned.)

<u>Activity #2</u>
    Distribute the materials students will use in this unit. Explain in detail how students are to use these materials.

    <u>Study Guides</u> Students should preview the study guide questions before each reading assignment to get a feeling for what events and ideas are important in that section. After reading the section, students will (as a class or individually) answer the questions to review the important events and ideas from that section of the book. Students should keep the study guides as study materials for the unit test.

    <u>Reading Assignment Sheet</u> You need to fill in the reading assignment sheet to let students know when their reading has to be completed. You can either write the assignment sheet on a side blackboard or bulletin board and leave it there for students to see each day, or you can duplicate copies for each student to have. In either case, you should advise students to become very familiar with the reading assignments so they know what is expected of them.

    <u>Extra Activities Center</u> The unit resource portion of this unit contains suggestions for a library of related books and articles in your classroom as well as crossword and word search puzzles. Make an extra activities center in your room where you will keep these materials for students to use. (Bring the books and articles in from the library and keep several copies of the puzzles on hand.) Explain to students that these materials are available for students to use when they finish reading assignments or other class work early.

Books Each school has its own rules and regulations regarding student use of school books. Advise students of the procedures that are normal for your school.

Activity #3

Explain that the novel is historical fiction. The author did research on the time period and the major historical figures and events mentioned in the novel. Then she used some of the facts and incorporated them in a fictional story. While there were many young male apprentices, there may or may not have been a boy named Johnny Tremain in Boston around the Revolutionary War era. Many of the events in the book are historical fact, such as the Boston Tea Party and the battle of Lexington and Concord. Encourage students to look for historical facts and fictional episodes as they read.

Activity #4

Show students how to preview the study questions and do the vocabulary work for Chapter I of Johnny Tremain. If students do not finish this assignment in class, they should complete it prior to the next class meeting.

Note: Make sure to talk about the picture at the beginning of each chapter before students read. After they read, they can refer to the picture again and see if they have any more information to add to what they said before reading.

LESSON TWO

Objectives
1. To read Chapter I
2. To review the main ideas and events from Chapter I
3. To introduce the Nonfiction assignment

Activity #1

You may want to read parts 1 and 2 of Chapter I aloud to the students to set the mood for the novel. Invite willing students to read aloud from parts 3-6.

Activity #2

Give the students time to answer the study guide questions, and then discuss the answers in detail. Write the answers on the board or overhead projector so students can have the correct answers for study purposes. Encourage students to take notes. If the students own their books, encourage them to use highlighter pens to mark important passages and the answers to the study guide questions.

Note: It is a good practice in public speaking and leadership skills for individual students to take charge of leading the discussion of the study questions. Perhaps a different student could go to the front of the class and lead the discussion each day that the study questions are discussed during this unit. Of course, the teacher should guide the discussion when appropriate and be sure to fill in any gaps the students leave.

Activity #3

Distribute copies of the Nonfiction Assignment sheet and go over it in detail with the students. Give them the due date for the assignment (Lesson 20.) Suggested topics for research are: life in the New England colonies in the 1700s; a biography of Paul Revere, Sam Adams, John Hancock, or Josiah Quincy; historical accounts of the Revolutionary War; child-rearing practices in colonial America; the silversmith trade; a history of the city of Boston and the state of Massachusetts.

KWL *Johnny Tremain*

Directions: Before reading, think about what you already know about Esther Forbes and/or *Johnny Tremain*. Write the information in the K column. Think about what you would like to find out from reading the book. Write your questions in the W column. After you have read the book, use the L column to write the answers to your questions from the W column, and anything else you remember from the book.

K **What I Know**	**W** **What I Want to Find Out**	**L** **What I Learned**

NONFICTION ASSIGNMENT SHEET
(To be completed after reading the required nonfiction article)

Name _____ Date _____ Class _____

Title of Nonfiction Read _____

Written By _____ Publication Date _____

I. Factual Summary: Write a short summary of the piece you read.

II. Vocabulary:
   1. With which vocabulary words in the piece did you encounter some degree of difficulty?

   2. How did you resolve your lack of understanding with these words?

III. Interpretation: What was the main point the author wanted you to get from reading his/her work?

IV. Criticism:
   1. With which points of the piece did you agree or find easy to accept? Why?

   2. With which points of the piece did you disagree or find difficult to believe? Why?

V. Personal Response: What do you think about this piece? OR How does this piece influence your ideas?

LESSON THREE

Objectives
    1. To do the prereading and vocabulary work for Chapter II
    2. To read Chapter II
    3. To give students practice reading orally
    4. To evaluate students' oral reading

Activity #1

    Give students about fifteen minutes to preview the study questions for Chapter II and do the related vocabulary work.

Activity #2

    Have students read Chapter II of *Johnny Tremain* out loud in class. You probably know the best way to get readers with your class; pick students at random, ask for volunteers, or use whatever method works best for your group. If you have not yet completed an oral reading evaluation for your students for this marking period, this would be a good opportunity to do so. A form is included with this unit for your convenience.

    If students do not complete reading Chapter II in class, they should do so prior to your next class meeting.

LESSON FOUR

Objectives
    1. To review the main ideas and events from Chapter II
    2. To preview the study questions for Chapter III
    3. To familiarize students with the vocabulary in Chapter III
    4. To read Chapter III

Activity #1

    Review the study questions from Chapter II. Choose different students to give their answers and explain them. Encourage students to record the correct answers on their study guide pages. If necessary, have them reread the text to locate information and verify their answers.

Activity #2

    Give students about fifteen minutes to preview the study questions for Chapter III and do the related vocabulary work.

Activity #3

    Have students read Chapter III for the rest of the period. If you have not completed the oral reading evaluations, do so now. If the evaluations have been completed, you may want the students to read silently. If students do not complete the reading assignment in class, they should do so prior to your next class meeting.

ORAL READING EVALUATION *Johnny Tremain*

Name_____Class_____Date_____

SKILL	EXCELLENT	GOOD	AVERAGE	FAIR	POOR
Fluency	5	4	3	2	1
Clarity	5	4	3	2	1
Audibility	5	4	3	2	1
Pronunciation	5	4	3	2	1
(other)	5	4	3	2	1
(other)	5	4	3	2	1

Total _____ Grade _____

Comments:

LESSON FIVE

Objectives
    1. To review the main ideas and events in Chapter III
    2. To give students the opportunity to practice writing a public service announcement
    3. To give the teacher the opportunity to evaluate each student's writing skills

Activity #1

    Review the study questions and answers for Chapter III. Tell students there will be a quiz on Chapters I, II, and III on the following class day.

Activity #2

    Distribute Writing Assignment #1 and discuss the directions in detail. Allow the remaining class time for students to work on the assignment. Give students an additional two or three days to complete the assignment, if necessary.

Activity #3

    Distribute copies of the Writing Evaluation Form (included in this Unit Plan.) Explain to students that during Lesson Nine you will be holding individual writing conferences about this writing assignment. Make sure they are familiar with the criteria on the Writing Evaluation Form.

Follow-Up: After you have graded the assignments, have a writing conference with each student, (This unit schedules one in Lesson Nine.) After the writing conference, allow students to revise their papers using your suggestions to complete the revision. I suggest grading the revisions on an A-C-E scale (all revisions well-done, some revisions made, few or no revisions made.) This will speed your grading time and still give some credit for the students' efforts.

LESSON SIX

Objectives
    1. To check students' comprehension of the events in Chapters I, II, and III
    2. To preview the study questions and vocabulary for Chapter IV
    3. To read Chapter IV silently

Activity #1
    Quiz--distribute quizzes (multiple choice study questions for Chapters I-III) and give students about ten minutes to complete them. Have students exchange papers. Grade the quizzes as a class. Collect the papers for recording the grades.

Activity #2
    Give students about fifteen minutes to do the prereading and vocabulary work for Chapter IV.

Activity #3
    Give students the remainder of the period to begin silently reading Chapter IV. Remind them that the reading must be completed prior to your next class meeting.

WRITING ASSIGNMENT 1
Johnny Tremain

PROMPT

When Johnny Tremain had an accident that leaves his hand crippled, many of the people he knew and cared for treated him differently. It was difficult for him to find work. He was very conscious of his handicap. Your assignment is to make a poster to help the people of Boston in 1775 become aware of handicaps, and how to treat people with handicaps.

PREWRITING

First decide on a theme for your poster. Then create a slogan--a catchy phrase stating your theme. Next, decide what your poster should look like. Do you want graphics--pictures, drawings, or photographs of handicapped people at work or play? Which handicaps will you portray? Spend some time looking at other public-service type posters and announcements to get ideas.

Decide on your audience. Who will you try to reach with your ad? How will following your suggestions benefit the handicapped and non-handicapped people who read your poster? Write a few short statements giving your ideas.

Make a rough layout of your poster. Make a sketch showing your slogan, the position of your copy (written words) and the graphics. You may have to do this several times before you are happy with it, so don't glue anything down!

DRAFTING

Write out the copy (words, written material) for your poster. You may need to revise this several times before you get the right feeling. You want to be brief and effective: say the most in the fewest words. Make sure to use powerful verbs and descriptive adjectives. Do the same thing with your slogan. Say it out loud or tape record it a few times to check out how it sounds. Again, you want it to be something that will spark the reader's interest. It should be long enough to say what you want, but short enough for the reader to remember. Use alliteration, onomatopoeia, or other literary devices to attract attention. Write it on paper when you like the way it sounds.

After you are happy with your copy, make a mock-up (pasted up rough draft) of your poster and see how things fit. You may want to use removable tacky-glue for this process. Make any necessary corrections. For example, if your copy is too long, shorten it to fit the space on your page. If your slogan takes up too much room, find synonyms to use to rephrase it and make it shorter. If the graphics look crowded, make them smaller or take a few out. Re-work your poster until you are satisfied with it.

PROMPT

When you finish the rough draft of your poster, ask another student to read it. After looking at your rough draft of the poster, he/she should tell you what he/she liked best about your work, which parts were difficult to understand, and ways in which your work could be improved. Review your poster considering your critic's comments, and make the corrections you think are necessary.

WRITING EVALUATION FORM *Johnny Tremain*

Name _____ Date _____ Class _____

Writing Assignment #1 for *Johnny Tremain*

Circle One For Each Item:

Slogan	excellent	good	fair	poor
Copy	excellent	good	fair	poor
Design	excellent	good	fair	poor
Graphics	excellent	good	fair	poor
Grammar	excellent	good	fair	poor (errors noted)
Spelling	excellent	good	fair	poor (errors noted)
Punctuation	excellent	good	fair	poor (errors noted)

Strengths:

Weaknesses:

Comments/Suggestions:

LESSON SEVEN

Objectives
    1. To review the main ideas and events in Chapter IV
    2. To complete the study questions and vocabulary for Chapter V
    3. To complete the reading for Chapter V

Activity #1

    Ask students if they thought the events in Chapter IV would turn out the way they did. Allow a few minutes for discussion. Then review the study questions and answers.

Activity #2

    Have students look at the picture and the title of Chapter V. Ask what they think it will be about. Then have them complete the vocabulary work and preview the study questions for Chapter V.

Activity #3

    Students may use the rest of the period to read the chapter. If possible, give them the choice of reading silently or reading aloud quietly with a partner.

LESSON EIGHT

Objectives
    1. To review the main ideas and events in Chapter V
    2. To complete the study questions and vocabulary for Chapter VI
    3. To complete the reading for Chapter VI

Activity #1

    Review the study questions and answers for Chapter V.

Activity #2

    Show students a clear glass jar of salt water and loose tea. Ask how tea is usually made, and why tea would be made with salt water. Then have students complete the vocabulary work and preview the study questions for Chapter VI.

Activity #3

    Students may use the rest of the period to read the chapter. If possible, give them the choice of reading silently or reading aloud quietly with a partner. Remind them that all reading must be completed before the next class period.

LESSON NINE

Objectives
1. To have students revise their first writing assignment
2. To give students time to work on their other reading and writing assignments

Activity #1
Call students to your desk (or some other private area) to discuss their posters from Writing Assignment #1. Use the completed Writing Evaluation Form as a basis for your critique.

Activity #2
Students should use this period (when they are not conferencing with you) to revise Writing Assignment #1 as necessary, or to work on silent reading and study guide questions.

LESSON TEN

Objectives
1. To review the main ideas and events from Chapter VI
2. To review for a quiz on Chapters IV-VII
3. To do the prereading and vocabulary work for Chapter VIII
4. To silently read Chapter VIII

Activity #1
Ask individual students to give the answers for the study guide questions for Chapter VI.

Activity #2
Ask students to get out their books and some paper (not their study guides.) Tell students to write down ten questions and answers which cover the main events and ideas in Chapters IV-VII. Discuss the students' questions and answers orally, making a list on the board of the questions with brief responses. Then review the study guide questions for those chapters, reminding students to get all of the answers in writing. Tell them they will have a quiz on Chapters IV-VII during the next class period.

Activity #3
Have students complete the vocabulary work and preview the study questions for Chapter VIII.

Activity #4
Allow students to use the rest of the period to either review for the quiz or read Chapter VIII.

LESSON ELEVEN

Objectives
1. To check students' understanding of the main ideas and events from Chapters IV-VII
2. To discuss the main ideas and events from Chapter VIII
3. To predict the answers to the study guide questions for Chapter IX
4. To preview the vocabulary for Chapter IX
5. To read Chapter IX

Activity #1
Use the multiple choice quiz/study guide questions from Chapters IV-VII. Choose one or several from each chapter for a quiz.

Activity #2
Discuss the answers to the study guide questions from Chapter VIII.

Activity #3
Distribute copies of the multiple choice quiz/study guide questions for Chapter IX. Encourage students to make predictions about the answers by circling or underlining the answer they think is correct.

Activity #4
Have the students read the chapters silently and compare their original predictions with the actual answers to the multiple choice questions. Remind them that any reading they do not finish in class must be done before the next class meeting.

LESSON TWELVE

Objectives
1. To give the students the opportunity to practice writing to persuade
2. To give the teacher the opportunity to evaluate the students' writing skills

Activity #1
Distribute Writing Assignment #2. Discuss the directions in detail and give students ample time to complete the assignment.

Activity #2
If time permits, you may allow several students to read their papers aloud in a debate format.

WRITING ASSIGNMENT #2
Johnny Tremain

PROMPT

You are a resident of Boston in 1774. The government in far-off England has been imposing taxes on your colony. You have no say in the laws or government. Some citizens are opposed to this method of government and want to change things (Whigs). Others support the King in England (Tories). Which side are you on? What can you say to a friend on the other side to convince him or her to change sides?

PREWRITING

You may want to read about the Whigs and Tories in a history book before forming your opinion. Make a list of the main beliefs and positions of each group. Number the points in order from most to least important. Then make a compare/contrast chart. Put one group on each side of the chart. For each Whig belief or position on the left side of the chart, write the corresponding Tory position on the right. Put these in order according to importance, with the most important at the top. You may use quotes and examples from history if they are accurate.

DRAFTING

Write out your argument. In the opening statement give your position. Use a paragraph for each point from your list. State your belief, tell why you believe it, give examples, and tell why you think the other point of view is in error. Summarize with a short statement of your opinion.

PROMPT

When you finish the rough draft, ask another student to look at it. You may want to read it aloud for the student, so it sounds like a real argument. After reading/listening, he or she should tell you what he/she liked best about your paper, which parts were difficult to understand or needed more information, and ways in which your work could be improved. Reread your paper considering your critic's comments and make the corrections you think are necessary.

PROOFREADING

Do a final proofreading of your paper, double-checking your grammar, spelling, organization, and the clarity of your ideas.

LESSON THIRTEEN

Objectives
    1. To review the main ideas and events in Chapter IX
    2. To complete the study questions and vocabulary for Chapter X
    3. To complete the reading for Chapter X

Activity #1
    Review the study questions and answers for Chapter IX.

Activity #2
    Give students ten or fifteen minutes to complete the prereading and vocabulary for Chapter X.

Activity #3
    You may want to read this chapter aloud for a change of pace. Encourage students to follow along in their books, or to close their eyes and visualize the action as they listen.

LESSON FOURTEEN

Objectives
    1. To review the main ideas and events in Chapter X
    2. To complete the study questions and vocabulary for Chapter XI
    3. To complete the reading for Chapter XI

Activity #1
    Review the study questions and answers for Chapter X.

Activity #2
    Give students ten or fifteen minutes to complete the prereading and vocabulary work for Chapter XI.

Activity #3
    Divide students into five groups, one for each section of the chapter. Have each group read one section and prepare a three minute report on it. Encourage them to use drawings in their reports. Go in order beginning with section 1 and have students give their reports.

LESSON FIFTEEN

Objectives
    1. To review the main ideas and events in Chapter XI
    2. To complete the study questions and vocabulary for Chapter XII
    3. To complete the reading for Chapter XII
    4. To review the main ideas and events in Chapter XII

Activity #1
    Review the study questions and answers for Chapter XI.

Activity #2
    Take a survey to see how students think the book will end. Write their predictions on the board. After reading, check and see how many made correct predictions.

Activity #3
    Students may use the rest of the period to read the chapter. If possible, give them the choice of reading silently or reading aloud quietly with a partner. Since this is a short chapter, they should be able to complete the reading in class.

Activity #4
    Have students complete the study guide questions with a partner and check the answers in their books. Go over the correct answers at the end of class.

LESSON SIXTEEN

Objective
> To discuss *Johnny Tremain* on interpretive and critical levels

Activity #1

Choose the questions from the Extra Writing Assignments/Discussion Questions which seem most appropriate for your students. A class discussion of these questions is most effective if students have been given the opportunity to formulate answers to the questions prior to the discussion. To this end, you may either have all the students formulate answers to all the questions, divide the class into groups and assign one or more questions to each group, or you could assign one question to each student in your class. The option you choose will make a difference in the amount of class time needed for this activity.

Activity #2

After students have had ample time to formulate answers to the questions, begin your class discussion of the questions and the ideas presented by the questions. Be sure students take notes during the discussion so they have information to study for the unit test.

EXTRA WRITING ASSIGNMENT/DISCUSSION QUESTIONS
Johnny Tremain

<u>Interpretation</u>

1. From what point of view is the story written? How does this affect our understanding of the story?

2. What insights into the life of the pre-Revolutionary War colonist does the author provide?

3. What are the main conflicts in the story? Are they resolved? If so, how? If not, why not?

4. What is the setting? How important is the setting to the story? Why?

5. Write a character sketch of one of the following: Johnny Tremain, Mr. Lapham, Rab, Cilla.

6. In Chapter II, why did Mrs. Lapham help Johnny work on Sunday when she knew it was against the law?

7. In Chapter III, what does Johnny's method of searching for new work tell us about his character?

8. What does the treatment Johnny receives after he injures his hand tell us about Isannah, Mrs. Lapham, Mr. Lapham, and the times in general?

9. In Chapter V, why does the author say that Johnny was expected to take to a life of crime?

10. In Chapter VIII, why didn't Johnny take his silver cup wit him?

11. In Chapter VIII, compare and contrast the viewpoints of James Otis and Sam Adams about the reasons for the war.

12. In Chapter IX, the author says that less attention was paid to the lower class workers at the Green Dragon than to the wealthy merchants who met at the *Boston Observer*. What does this tell about the society of the times?

13. In Chapter X, why were Billy Dawes and his wife laughing as he got ready to leave?

14. In Chapter XII, why were the townspeople whistling Yankee Doodle?

15. Why did Mrs. Lapham let Lavinia Lyte take her two girls?

16. Why do you think Lavinia Lyte was interested in Isannah?

Extra Discussion Questions *Johnny Tremain*

<u>Critical</u>

17. Do the chapter titles add to the effectiveness of the book? Why or why not?

18. Which characters were best developed?

19. Which characters were least developed? Why?

20. How did Johnny change over the course of the novel? Were these changes for the better?

21. Compare and contrast Johnny's visit to the Laphams in Chapter III with his visit in Chapter VII.

22. Why was the debate between Otis and Adams important to the story?

23. Which events were historical, and which were fictional? Was the history accurately portrayed?

24. Was the character of Johnny believable?

25. Compare and contrast child rearing practices at the time of the book with those of today.

26. Compare and contrast the treatment of the handicapped at the time of the book with that of today.

<u>Personal Response</u>

27. Did you enjoy reading Johnny Tremain? Why or why not?

28. Would you have liked to live in Boston in 1773-1776? Why or why not?

29. Who was your favorite character in the book? Why?

30. Have you read any other stories similar to Johnny Tremain? If so, tell about them.

31. How did you feel when people rejected Johnny because of his injured hand?

32. What do you think Johnny will do next?

QUOTATIONS *Johnny Tremain*

Discuss the significance of the following quotations.

1. 'I, Johnny Tremain . . . swear from this day onward . . . to walk more humbly and modestly before God and man.'

2. 'Your master made that creamer--forty years ago. He made the entire set.'

3. 'I never do. I don't hold much with these fellows that are always trying to stir up trouble between us and England. Maybe English rule ain't always perfect, but it's good enough for me.'

4. 'No. My baptized Bible name is Jonathan. I've always been called Johnny. That's the way my papers were made out to your grandpa. I am Jonathan Lyte Tremain.'

5. 'Tell your master I'll pay a bit more than is usual for you. Don't let him shunt one of those other boys off on me.'

6. 'You're getting above yourself--like I tried to point out to you. God is going to send you a dire punishment for your pride.'

7. 'My! That's worse than anything I had imagined. Now isn't that a shame! Bright boy like Johnny just ruined. No more good than a horse with sprung knees.'

8. 'It has. If I have to, I'll wait ten years to get that Dove.'

9. 'Run away, boy, run away. You knew you could not do the work and yet you came and took up my valuable time and . . . '

10. 'It's about like dancing . . . keeping rhythm. You'll learn right off. Of course you'll be scared, but just remember this: no matter how scared you are, he's more so.'

11. 'Johnny Tremain is a bold fellow. I knew he could learn--if he didn't get killed first. It was sink or swim for him--and happens he's swimming.'

12. 'Why do you go out of your way to make bad feeling?'

13. 'It is you who put the idea in their heads. You know you usually go about with that hand in your pocket, looking as if you had an imp of Hell hidden away, and then someone asks you and you pull it out with a slow flourish, as if you said, "This is the most disgusting thing you ever saw." No wonder you scare everybody. Tonight happens you just forgot.'

14. 'Yes, God give us strength to resist. That tea cannot be allowed to land.'

15. 'Without you, there would not have been any belief in liberty to lose. I will, as always, do anything--everything you wish.'

16. 'If I had to hurt my hand. I'm glad it was while doing something worth while--not merely mending an old spoon.'

17. 'Here's to December the sixteenth.'

18. 'Well boys, you've had a fine, pleasant evening for your Indian caper, haven't you? But mind . . . you've got to pay the fiddler yet.'

19. 'Now boys, you forget talk like that. You remember that we don't like being here in Boston any better than you like having us. I'd rather be with my wife and children in Bath. We're both in a tight spot. But if we keep our tempers and you keep your tempers, why, we can fix things between us somehow. We're all one people, you know.'

20. 'Miss Lavinia is about making a monkey out of Isannah.'

21. 'No. This is the end. The end of one thing--the beginning of something else. They won't come back because there is going to be a war--a civil war. And we'll win. First folk like them get routed out of Milton--then out of Boston. And the cards are going to be reshuffled. Dealt again . . . Shall I shutter the kitchen too?'

22. 'No. That time is past. I will work for war: the complete freedom of these colonies from any European power. We can have that freedom only by fighting for it.'

23. 'We give all we have, lives, property, safety, skills . . . we fight, we die, for a simple thing. Only that a man can stand up.'

24. 'You know, my father had to fly France because of the tyranny over there. He was only a child. But now, in a way, I'm fighting for that child . . . that no frightened lost child ever is sent out a refugee from his own country because of race or religion.'

25. 'Disperse, ye rebels, ye villains, disperse! Why don't ye lay down your arms?'

26. 'They've begun it. We'll end it, but this war . . . it may last quite a long time.'

27. 'Isannah is going with me. Your mother has too many kittens.'

28. 'It is just as James Otis said. We are fighting, partly, for just that. Because a man is a private is no reason he should be treated like cordwood.'

29. 'You can have that musket. I sort of like to think of its going on. I've put a better stock on it, changed the angle of the steel. Look at that flint. The one it had was too smooth. I've knapped it.'

30. 'Yes, and some if us would die--so other men can stand up on their feet like men. A great many are going to die for that. They have in the past. They will a hundred years from now--two hundred. God grant there will always be good enough. Men like Rab.'

31. 'No need. I can hold it still myself.'

LESSON SEVENTEEN

Objectives
1. To give the students the opportunity to practice writing to inform
2. To give the teacher the opportunity to evaluate the students' writing skills

Activity #1

Distribute Writing Assignment #3 Discuss the directions in detail and give students ample time to complete the assignment.

Note: You may want to assign this as a group project and assign one event or chapter of the book to each group to avoid overlap.

Activity #2

If time permits, you may allow several students to assemble their articles into a class newspaper.

LESSON EIGHTEEN

Objectives
1. To give the students time to research their non-fiction assignments
2. To instruct the students on the proper use of the library

Activity #1

Take the students to the school library to work on their non-fiction assignments. Assist them as necessary.

Activity #2

Students who have completed their non-fiction assignments should use the time to work on other reading or writing assignments.

WRITING ASSIGNMENT #3
Johnny Tremain

PROMPT

Congratulations! You have just been hired as a roving reporter for the *Boston Observer*. Many exciting things are going on in Boston right now (between the years 1773 and 1775). Your job is to write a news report on one of the events. You may cover the event from a news angle (mostly reporting the facts), or you may cover it from a human interest angle (giving more detail about the people involved.)

PREWRITING

The first thing you need to do is choose an event to write about. Skim through *Johnny Tremain* and find an event or a scene from the book that is especially interesting to you. Read it again and see if there is enough information to make it into a news article.

A news article must answer six basic questions: **who** is the story about; **what** happened; **when** did it happen; **where** did it happen, **why** did it happen, and **how** did the event occur? These are called the 5W and H questions. Make a list of these questions and answer them based on the information in the book.

Once you have answered the 5W and H questions, decide on their order of importance for your story. Number them on your list.

DRAFTING

Write a rough draft of your news story. Check your list to make sure you have included all of the information. Make sure you put the most important information from your list first in the story. Then create the headline. The headline tells the main idea of the story. It usually includes who is in the story and what happened. A headline does not have to be a complete sentence, but it should have a powerful verb. Read some headlines in your local newspaper to get the idea before you write yours. Next, put your byline and dateline on the news article. The byline is the name of the writer. It goes under the headline, on the right side of the page. The dateline is the date and place where the story took place. It goes on the first line of the story, before the story begins.

PROOFREADING

When you finish the rough draft, ask another student to look at it. You may want to give the student your checklist so he/she can double check for you and see that you have included all of the information. After reading, he or she should tell you what he/she liked best about your news article, which parts were difficult to understand or needed more information, and ways in which your work could be improved. Reread your news article considering your critic's comments and make the corrections you think are necessary.

LESSON NINETEEN

Objectives
1. To watch the movie or listen to the audio version of the book
2. To compare and contrast the media version with the book

Activity #1
Show the movie version of Johnny Tremain. It is available through several educational media services, and also at commercial video stores. Depending on your students, you may want to have them take notes while they are watching, to jot down the scenes where the movie and book differ.

Activity #2
Listen to the audio cassette version of the book. If students listen to the abridged version, have them jot down the scenes from the book that are included on the audio tape.

Activity #3
Have a discussion comparing and contrasting the book with either the audio or video version. You may want to make a Venn diagram on the board and record the points the students make during their discussion.

LESSON TWENTY

Objectives
1. To widen the breadth of students' knowledge about the topics discussed or touched upon in *Johnny Tremain*
2. To check students' non-fiction assignments

Activity
Ask each student to give a brief oral report about the nonfiction work he/she read for the nonfiction assignment. Your criteria for evaluating this report will vary depending on the level of your students. You may wish for students to give a complete report without using notes of any kind, or you may want students to read directly from a written report, or you may want to do something in between these two extremes. Just make students aware of your criteria in ample time for them to prepare their reports.

Start with one student's report, After that, ask if anyone else in the class has read on a topic related to the first student's report. If no one has, choose another student at random. After each report, be sure to ask if anyone has a report related to the one just completed. That will help keep a continuity during the discussion of the reports.

LESSON TWENTY ONE

Objective
> To review all of the vocabulary work done in this unit

VOCABULARY REVIEW ACTIVITIES

1. Divide your class into two teams and have an old-fashioned spelling or definition bee.

2. Give each of your students (or students in groups of two, three or four) a *Johnny Tremain* Vocabulary Word Search Puzzle. The person (group) to find all of the vocabulary words in the puzzle first wins.

3. Give students a Vocabulary Word Search Puzzle without the word list. The person or group to find the most vocabulary words in the puzzle wins.

4. Use a *Johnny Tremain* Vocabulary Crossword Puzzle. Put the puzzle onto a transparency on the overhead projector (so everyone can see it), and do the puzzle together as a class.

5. Give students a *Johnny Tremain* Vocabulary Matching Worksheet to do.

6. Divide your class into two teams. Use the *Johnny Tremain* vocabulary words with their letters jumbled as a word list. Student 1 from Team A faces off against Student 1 from Team B. You write the first jumbled word on the board. The first student (1A or 1B) to unscramble the word wins the chance for his/her team to score points. If 1A wins the jumble, go to student 2A and give him/her a definition. He/she must give you the correct spelling of the vocabulary word which fits that definition. If he/she does, Team A scores a point, and you give student 3A a definition for which you expect a correctly spelled matching vocabulary word. Continue giving Team A definitions until some team member makes an incorrect response. An incorrect response sends the game back to the jumbled-word face off, this time with students 2A and 2B. Instead of repeating giving definitions to the first few students of each team, continue with the student after the one who gave the last incorrect response on the team. For example, if Team B wins the jumbled-word face-off, and student 5B gave the last incorrect answer for Team B, you would start this round of definition questions with student 6B, and so on. The team with the most points wins!

7. Have students write a story in which they correctly use as many vocabulary words as possible. Have students read their compositions orally. Post the most original compositions on your bulletin board!

8. Have students draw pictures to illustrate the vocabulary words. Let the other students guess what the word is.

LESSON TWENTY TWO

Objective
　　To review the main ideas presented in *Johnny Tremain*

Activity #1
　　Choose one of the review games/activities included in the packet and spend your class period as outlined there.

Activity #2
　　Remind students of the date for the Unit Test. Stress the review of the Study Guides and their class notes as a last minute, brush-up review for homework.

REVIEW GAMES / ACTIVITIES

1. Ask the class to make up a unit test for *Johnny Tremain*. The test should have 4 sections: multiple choice, true/false, short answer and essay. Students may use 1/2 period to make the test, including a separate answer sheet, and then swap papers and use the other 1/2 class period to take a test a classmate has devised. (open book)

2. Take 1/2 period for students to make up true and false questions (including the answers). Collect the papers and divide the class into two teams. Draw a big tic-tac-toe board on the chalk board. Make one team X and one team O. Ask questions to each side, giving each student one turn. If the question is answered correctly, that student's team's letter (X or O) is placed in the box. If the answer is incorrect, no mark is placed in the box. The object is to get three marks in a row like tic-tac-toe. You may want to keep track of the number of games won for each team.

3. Take 1/2 period for students to make up questions (true/false and short answer). Collect the questions. Divide the class into two teams. You'll alternate asking questions to individual members of teams A & B, like in a spelling bee. The question keeps going from A to B until it is correctly answered, then a new question is asked. A correct answer does not allow the team to get another question. Correct answers are +2 points; incorrect answers are -1 point.

4. Allow students time to quiz each other (in pairs) from their study guides and class notes.

5. Give students a *Johnny Tremain* crossword puzzle to complete.

REVIEW GAMES / ACTIVITIES

6. Divide your class into two teams. Use the *Johnny Tremain* crossword words with their letters jumbled as a word list. Student 1 from Team A faces off against Student 1 from Team B. You write the first jumbled word on the board. The first student (1A or 1B) to unscramble the word wins the chance for his/her team to score points. If 1A wins the jumble, go to student 2A and give him/her a clue. He/she must give you the correct word which matches that clue. If he/she does, Team A scores a point, and you give student 3A a clue for which you expect another correct response. Continue giving Team A clues until some team member makes an incorrect response. An incorrect response sends the game back to the jumbled-word face off, this time with students 2A and 2B. Instead of repeating giving clues to the first few students of each team, continue with the student after the one who gave the last incorrect response on the team.

7. Take on the persona of "The Answer Person." Allow students to ask any question about the book. Answer the questions, or tell students where to look in the book to find the answer.

8. Students may enjoy playing charades with events from the story. Select a student to start. Give him/her a card with a scene or event from the story. Allow the players to use their books to find the scene being described. The first person to guess each charade performs the next one.

9. Play a categories-type quiz game. A master is included in this Unit Plan. Make an overhead transparency of the categories form. Divide the class into teams of three or four players each. Have each team choose a recorder and a banker. Choose a team to go first. That team will choose a category and point amount. Ask the question to the entire class. Use the Study Guide Quiz and Vocabulary questions. Give the teams one minute to discuss the answer and write it down. Walk around the room and check the answers. Each team that answers correctly receives the points. 78
Incorrect answers are not penalized; they just don't receive any points. Cross out that square on the playing board. Play continues until all squares have been used. The winning team is the one with the most points. You can assign bonus points to any square or squares you choose.

10. Have students complete the last column (What I Learned) of the KWL sheet you distributed in Lesson One. Discuss their answers with the class.

11. Play a "Pictionary" type game. Divide the class into teams. Each team makes a simple line drawing of a scene from the story. The other team or teams try to describe the scene. You may want to allow students to use their books to verify their guesses.

QUIZ GAME
Johnny Tremain

Chapters I, II	Chapters III, IV	Chapters V, VI	Chapters VII, VIII	Chapters IX, X	Chapters XI, XII
100	100	100	100	100	100
200	200	200	200	200	200
300	300	300	300	300	300
400	400	400	400	400	400
500	500	500	500	500	500

LESSON TWENTY THREE

Objective
To test the students' understanding of the main ideas and themes in *Johnny Tremain*

Activity #1
Distribute the *Johnny Tremain* Unit Tests. Go over the instructions in detail and allow the students the entire class period to complete the exam.

Activity #2
Collect all test papers and assigned books prior to the end of the class period.

NOTES ABOUT THE UNIT TESTS IN THIS UNIT:

There are 5 different unit tests which follow.

There are two short answer tests which are based primarily on facts from the novel. The answer key for short answer unit test 1 follows the student test. The answer key for short answer test 2 follows the student short answer unit test 2.

There is one advanced short answer unit test. It is based on the extra discussion questions. Use the matching key for short answer unit test 2 to check the matching section of the advanced short answer unit test. There is no key for the short answer questions. The answers will be based on the discussions you have had during class.

There are two multiple choice unit tests. Following the two unit tests, you will find an answer sheet on which students should mark their answers. The same answer sheet should be used for both tests; however, students' answers will be different for each test. Following the students' answer sheet for the multiple choice tests you will find your answer keys.

The short answer tests have a vocabulary section. You should choose 20 of the vocabulary words from this unit, read them orally and have the students write them down. Then, either have students write a definition or use the words in sentences.

UNIT TESTS

SHORT ANSWER UNIT TEST 1 *Johnny Tremain*

I. Matching/ Identify

____ 1. Johnny Tremain   A. befriended Johnny and heard his story
____ 2. Rab   B. said he would work for war
____ 3. Paul Revere   C. colonists loyal to England
____ 4. Mr. Lorne   D. organized spy system
____ 5. John Hancock   E. silversmith apprentice/Observer Club messenger
____ 6. Sam Adams   F. wealthy merchant and Whig leader
____ 7. James Otis   G. Johnny's great-uncle, owner of silver cups
____ 8. Tories   H. said "so a man can stand up"
____ 9. Whigs   I. colonist who wanted freedom from England
____ 10. Mr. Lyte   J. owned the *Boston Observer*

II. Short Answer

1. What did Johnny tell Cilla about his middle name and his childhood?

2. Describe Johnny's accident, including who was responsible for it, and what the result was.

Short Answer Unit Test 1 continued *Johnny Tremain*

3. Describe the main events and outcome of Johnny's trial.

4. What was the grievance the Boston colonists had with England in the fall of 1773?

5. Describe the events of the night of December 16, 1773.

6. Describe the relationship between Johnny and Lieutenant Stranger.

Short Answer Unit Test 1 continued *Johnny Tremain*

7. What was the plan to warn the men in Lexington and Concord? How had Johnny helped with the plan?

8. What id Lavinia Lyte tell Johnny about his background before she left for England?

9. What was Johnny's observation as he watched the boats full of wounded British privates and officers being unloaded?

10. How did the story end?

Short Answer Unit Test 1 continued *Johnny Tremain*

III. Essay

What are the main conflicts in the story? Are they resolved? If not, why not?

Short Answer Unit Test 1 continued *Johnny Tremain*

IV. Vocabulary

Listen to the vocabulary words and spell them. After you have spelled all the words, go back and write down the definitions.

WORD	**DEFINITION**
1.	
2.	
3.	
4.	
5.	
6.	
7.	
8.	
9.	
10.	
11.	
12.	
13.	
14.	
15.	
16.	
17.	
18.	
19.	
20.	

ANSWER KEY SHORT ANSWER UNIT TEST 1 *Johnny Tremain*

I. Matching/ Identify

E	1.	Johnny Tremain	A.	befriended Johnny and heard his story
A	2.	Rab	B.	said he would work for war
D	3.	Paul Revere	C.	colonists loyal to England
J	4.	Mr. Lorne	D.	organized spy system
F	5.	John Hancock	E.	silversmith apprentice/Observer Club messenger
B	6.	Sam Adams	F.	wealthy merchant and Whig leader
H	7.	James Otis	G.	Johnny's great-uncle, owner of silver cups
C	8.	Tories	H.	said "so a man can stand up"
I	9.	Whigs	I.	colonist who wanted freedom from England
G	10.	Mr. Lyte	J.	owned the *Boston Observer*

II. Short Answer

1. What did Johnny tell Cilla about his middle name and his childhood?

    He told her his middle name was Lyte. His mother was kin to Jonathan Lyte. She gave him the silver cup with the L monogram when she died, and told him to go to Mr. Lyte if he "got to the end of everything."

2. Describe Johnny's accident, including who was responsible for it, and what the result was.

    Dove gave Johnny a cracked crucible for melting the silver. As Johnny was reaching out to get the silver he slipped in beeswax that was on the floor. His right hand came down on top of the furnace, and was severely burned. He was ill for several days. Mrs. Lapham treated him as best she could, but when he recovered he found that the thumb and palm had drawn together, and the hand was useless.

3. Describe the main events and outcome of Johnny's trial.

    Mr. Lyte told his version, insisting that Johnny was a thief and should get the death penalty. Then Mr. Quincy had Johnny tell his story. After that, he put Cilla on the stand. She confirmed Johnny's story. As she was finishing, Isannah ran into the courtroom, flung herself at the Justice, and gave her account of the Johnny's story. The Justice dismissed the case, saying there was no evidence that Johnny had stolen the cup, or that Johnny's cup was the one that had been stolen. He gave the one cup back to Johnny. Isannah kissed Johnny's burned hand while they were standing on the sidewalk outside of the courthouse.

4. What was the grievance the Boston colonists had with England in the fall of 1773?

> There was a tax on tea. The colonists insisted they would not be taxed if they could not vote for the men who taxed them.

5. Describe the events of the night of December 16, 1773.

> The disguised boys, and Paul Revere, boarded the ships. They chopped open the wooden tea chests, then opened the canvas bags and dumped the tea into the harbor. They didn't damage any of the other cargo. After the tea had all been dumped, they cleaned the decks of the ships. Many people stood on the shore watching. When the last of the tea had been dumped, they all shouted a hurrah. The British Admiral Montague shouted from a window that they would all have to pay the fiddler.

6. Describe the relationship between Johnny and Lieutenant Stranger.

> They were equals when riding, and Johnny worshipped him. Stranger enjoyed having a worthwhile student. Once indoors, Stranger was a gentleman and a British officer and Johnny was his inferior.

7. What was the plan to warn the men in Lexington and Concord? How had Johnny helped with the plan?

> Bentley and Richardson rowed Paul Revere across the river to Charlestown. Then Paul Revere rode to Lexington and Concord. Meanwhile, Robert Newman hung two lanterns in the tower at Christ Church. Billy Dawes got out through the gates of the city by pretending to be a drunkard selling a horse. Johnny had found OUT the news of the campaign by sea from Dove, and warned the men.

8. What did Lavinia Lyte tell Johnny about his background before she left for England?

> She told him that Mr. Lyte truly believed Johnny was an impostor, as one of his cups had been stolen and a young boy was used to pretend to be a relative. Johnny's mother was Vinnie Lyte. She married a naval surgeon and prisoner of war named Dr. Charles Latour. The family was against the marriage because he was a French Catholic. They went to France, where he died. Latour's family sent Vinnie to a convent, where Johnny was born. When Lavinia saw Johnny she did some investigating and found out the whole story. Lavinia told Johnny he could call her Aunt Lavinia.

9. What was Johnny's observation as he watched the boats full of wounded British privates and officers being unloaded?

> He noticed that the boats with officers had only a few on board, and they were unloaded first. The boats with the privates on them were crowded and were left until last. The wounded privates were not treated well. Johnny thought it was not right to mistreat a man because he was of a lower rank.

10. How did the story end?
   Johnny went outside of the tavern to get fresh air while the doctor was getting his instruments ready. He heard the distant sound of "Yankee Doodle." He saw a line of men marching, and behind them was Rab's grandfather. Johnny started to run after him to tell him of Rab's death, but stopped himself.

SHORT ANSWER UNIT TEST 2 *Johnny Tremain*

1. Matching/ Identify

_____ 1. Rab   A. owner of *Boston Observer*
_____ 2. Cilla   B. greedy merchant/Johnny's great-uncle
_____ 3. Lieutenant Stranger   C. taught Johnny to ride well
_____ 4. Johnny Tremain   D. treated Johnny's burned hand
_____ 5. Mr. Lyte   E. said "that a man can stand up"
_____ 6. Sam Adams   F. warned Lexington and Concord of battle
_____ 7. Paul Revere   G. befriended Johnny and listened to his story
_____ 8. Dr. Warren   H. silversmith apprentice/Observer Club messenger
_____ 9. Mr. Lorne   I. said he would fight for war
_____ 10. James Otis   J. Lapham daughter intended to marry Johnny

II. Short Answer

1. Describe Johnny's accident, including who was responsible for it, and what the result was.

2. Describe Johnny's visit to the Lyte mansion when he took his cup to Mr. Lyte.

Short Answer Unit Test 2 continued *Johnny Tremain*

3. How did Johnny, under Rab's guidance, beginning to change, and what were the results?

4. What plan for the tea was developed in the attic at the Boston Observer? Who was the spokesperson and one of the creators of the plan?

5. What event had the Boston Observers Club members upset? What did they do in response?

6. What information did Johnny get from Lydia? What happened as a result of his passing on the information?

Short Answer Unit Test 2 continued *Johnny Tremain*

7. Describe the feeling and scene in Boston after the battle at Lexington.

8. What did Lavinia Lyte tell Johnny before she left for England?

9. Describe Johnny's last meeting with Rab.

10. What did Dr. Warren offer to do for Johnny, and what was Johnny's reply?

Short Answer Unit Test 2 continued *Johnny Tremain*

III. Essay

Write a character sketch of Johnny.

Short Answer Unit Test 2 continued *Johnny Tremain*

IV. Vocabulary

Listen to the vocabulary words and spell them. After you have spelled all the words, go back and write down the definitions.

WORD	DEFINITION
1.	
2.	
3.	
4.	
5.	
6.	
7.	
8.	
9.	
10.	
11.	
12.	
13.	
14.	
15.	
16.	
17.	
18.	
19.	
20.	

ANSWER KEY SHORT ANSWER UNIT TEST 2 *Johnny Tremain*

I. Matching/ Identify
Use this answer key for Short Answer Unit Test 2 and the Advanced Short Answer Unit Test.

G	1.	Rab	A.	owner of *Boston Observer*
J	2.	Cilla	B.	greedy merchant/Johnny's great-uncle
C	3.	Lieutenant Stranger	C.	taught Johnny to ride well
H	4.	Johnny Tremain	D.	treated Johnny's burned hand
B	5.	Mr. Lyte	E.	said "that a man can stand up"
I	6.	Sam Adams	F.	warned Lexington and Concord of battle
F	7.	Paul Revere	G.	befriended Johnny and listened to his story
D	8.	Dr. Warren	H.	silversmith apprentice/Observer Club messenger
A	9.	Mr. Lorne	I.	said he would fight for war
E	10.	James Otis	J.	Lapham daughter intended to marry Johnny

II. Short Answer

1. Describe Johnny's accident, including who was responsible for it, and what the result was.
    Dove gave Johnny a cracked crucible for melting the silver. As Johnny was reaching out to get the silver he slipped in beeswax that was on the floor. His right hand came down on top of the furnace, and was severely burned. He was ill for several days. Mrs. Lapham treated him as best she could, but when he recovered he found that the thumb and palm had drawn together, and the hand was useless.

2. Describe Johnny's visit to the Lyte mansion when he took his cup to Mr. Lyte.
    Twelve people from the family were gathered in the drawing room. They went into the dining room to look at the three silver cups on the sideboard. Johnny gave his cup to Mr. Lyte, who compared it to one of his own. Then he accused Johnny of having stolen the cup. He ordered the sheriff, who was also there, to arrest Johnny.

3. How did Johnny, under Rab's guidance, beginning to change, and what were the results?
    He began spending his time reading, learning to write with his left hand, and exercising his horse. Rab talked to him about his rude manners and Johnny began to watch himself. He discovered that politeness had rewards. Whenever he went to Mr. Adams's house he was invited in, and Mr. Adams began to employ him to do express riding for the Boston Committee of Correspondence.

4. What plan for the tea was developed in the attic at the Boston Observer? Who was the spokesperson and one of the creators of the plan?

   Sam Adams told the others about the plan. Rab and Paul Revere would find about thirty young men and boys to throw the tea on the ships overboard into Boston Harbor. They were to dress like Indians so they would not be recognized.

5. What event had the Boston Observers Club members upset? What did they do in response?

   General Gage had taken the cannon and gunpowder from Charlestown and the Minute Men had not even known about it until it was too late. The club members set up a spy network to make sure they knew what the British were doing.

6. What information did Johnny get from Lydia? What happened as a result of his passing on the information?

   The British were planning to take Portsmouth. Paul Revere warned the men and they seized the British stores instead.

7. Describe the feeling and scene in Boston after the battle at Lexington.

   The British troops were restless. The local people were wondering what was going on because so many Marines and other troops were moving in and out. General Gage sent for Hancock and the others, but they had already left Boston. There was a general feeling of tension and excitement.

8. What did Lavinia Lyte tell Johnny before she left for England?

   She told him that Mr. Lyte truly believed Johnny was an impostor, as one of his cups had been stolen and a young boy was used to pretend to be a relative. Johnny's mother was Vinnie Lyte. She married a naval surgeon and prisoner of war named Dr. Charles Latour. The family was against the marriage because he was a French Catholic. They went to France, where he died. Latour's family sent Vinnie to a convent, where Johnny was born. When Lavinia saw Johnny she did some investigating and found out the whole story. Lavinia told Johnny he could call her Aunt Lavinia.

9. Describe Johnny's last meeting with Rab.

   Rab was in Buckman's Tavern. He gave his musket to Johnny, and asked him to go to Silsbee's Cove to see his family. While Johnny was in the room, Rab pretended to be better than he really was. Rab asked Johnny to go to Silsbee's Cove to check on his family.

10. What did Dr. Warren offer to do for Johnny, and what was Johnny's reply?

    Dr. Warren offered to cut through the scar tissue so Johnny could use his injured hand to hold a musket. Johnny accepted the offer.

ADVANCED SHORT ANSWER TEST *Johnny Tremain*

I. Matching/Identify

_____ 1. Rab   A. owner of *Boston Observer*
_____ 2. Cilla   B. greedy merchant/Johnny's great-uncle
_____ 3. Lieutenant Stranger   C. taught Johnny to ride well
_____ 4. Johnny Tremain   D. treated Johnny's burned hand
_____ 5. Mr. Lyte   E. said "that a man can stand up"
_____ 6. Sam Adams   F. warned Lexington and Concord of battle
_____ 7. Paul Revere   G. befriended Johnny and listened to his story
_____ 8. Dr. Warren   H. silversmith apprentice/Observer Club messenger
_____ 9. Mr. Lorne   I. said he would fight for war
_____ 10. James Otis   J. Lapham daughter intended to marry Johnny

II. Short Answer

1. What insights into the life of the pre-Revolutionary War colonists does the author provide?

2. What are the main conflicts in the story? Are they resolved? If so, how? If not, why not?

Advanced Short Answer Test continued *Johnny Tremain*

3. Do the chapter titles add to the effectiveness of the book? Why or why not?

4. How did Johnny change over the course of the novel? Were these changes for the better?

5. Why was the debate between James Otis and Sam Adams important to the story?

Advanced Short Answer Test continued *Johnny Tremain*

III. Quotations

Explain the importance of the following quotations.

1. 'No, my baptized Bible name is Jonathan. I've always been called Johnny. That's the way my papers were made out to your grandpa. I am Jonathan Lyte Tremain.'

2. 'Why do you go out of your way to make bad feeling?'

3. 'No, this is the end. The end of one thing--the beginning of something else. They won't come back because there is going to be a war--a civil war. And we'll win. First folk like them get routed out of Milton--then out of Boston. And the cards are going to be reshuffled. Dealt again . . . Shall I shutter the kitchen too?'

Advanced Short t Answer Test continued *Johnny Tremain*

4. 'We give all we have, lives, property, safety, skills . . . we fight, we die, for a simple thing. Only that a man can stand up.'

5. 'Isannah is going with me. Your mother has too many kittens.'

Advanced Short Answer Unit Test *Johnny Tremain*

IV. Vocabulary

   Listen to the vocabulary words and write them down. After you have written down all of the words, write a paragraph in which you use all of the words. The paragraph must relate in some way to *Johnny Tremain*.

MULTIPLE CHOICE UNIT TEST 1 *Johnny Tremain*

I. Matching/ Identify

____ 1. Johnny Tremain   A. befriended Johnny and heard his story
____ 2. Rab   B. said he would work for war
____ 3. Paul Revere   C. colonists loyal to England
____ 4. Mr. Lorne   D. organized spy system
____ 5. John Hancock   E. silversmith apprentice/Observer Club messenger
____ 6. Sam Adams   F. wealthy merchant and Whig leader
____ 7. James Otis   G. Johnny's great-uncle, owner of silver cups
____ 8. Tories   H. said "so a man can stand up"
____ 9. Whigs   I. colonist who wanted freedom from England
____ 10. Mr. Lyte   J. owned the *Boston Observer*

II. Multiple Choice

1. True or False: Johnny told Cilla his middle name was Lyte. His mother was related to Jonathan Lyte. She gave him the silver cup with the L monogram when she died, and told him to go to Mr. Lyte if he "got to the end of everything."
    A. True
    B. False

2. Which of the following statements does **not** describe Johnny's accident?
    A. Dove gave Johnny a cracked crucible for melting the silver.
    B. As Johnny was reaching out to get the silver he slipped in beeswax that was on the floor.
    C. His right hand came down on top of the furnace, and was severely burned.
    D. When he recovered he found that his first three fingers had drawn together, and the hand was useless.

3. Which of the following did **not** happen at the trial?
    A. Mr. Lyte asked for leniency for Johnny, and said he only wanted his cup back.
    B. Cilla took the stand and confirmed Johnny's story.
    C. The Justice said there was no evidence that Johnny had stolen the cup.
    D. Isannah kissed Johnny's burned had outside the courthouse.

Multiple Choice Unit Test 1 continued *Johnny Tremain*

4. What was the grievance the colonists had with England in the Fall of 1773?
    A. All boys over the age of thirteen had to go to England to serve in the Army. The townspeople didn't want their young men to go.
    B. The people were not allowed to worship as they pleased. They all had to belong to the Church of England.
    C. All mail in and out of Boston was inspected by the British soldiers. The colonist said this was an invasion of their privacy.
    D. There was a tax on tea. The colonists insisted they would not be taxed if they could not vote for the men who taxed them.

5. What plan was developed in the attic at the *Boston Observer*?
    A. The tea would be stolen and given to the citizens.
    B. The tea would be burned, along with the ships.
    C. The tea on the ships was to be thrown overboard into Boston Harbor.
    D. The ships would be moved to the ocean and sunk.

6. Why did Johnny and Rab put up with Dove?
    A. They thought he might be able to give them valuable information from the British army.
    B. Johnny was still plotting he revenge for Dove's part in his accident.
    C. Mr. Lorne said they had to be kind to everyone.
    D. Dove had a lot of money and treated them to food and entertainment.

7. Whose relationship is being described here? They were equals when riding, and Johnny worshipped him. He enjoyed having a worthwhile student. Once indoors, he was a gentleman and an officer and Johnny was his inferior.
    A. Johnny and Earl Percy
    B. Johnny and Colonel Smith
    C. Johnny and General Gage
    D. Johnny and Lieutenant Stranger

8. Which of the following statements was **not** part of what Lavinia Lyte told Johnny?
    A. Mr. Lyte knew Johnny was telling the truth, but didn't want to admit it.
    B. Johnny's mother was Vinnie Lyte. She married Dr. Charles Latour.
    C. Johnny's father died in France.
    D. Vinnie's maid arranged for her and Johnny to return to America.

Multiple Choice Unit Test 1 continued *Johnny Tremain*

9. What was Johnny's observation as he watched the boats full of wounded British soldiers being unloaded?
    A. He thought the bloodshed was a terrible waste of lives on both sides.
    B. The wounded officers and privates were treated differently. He thought this was unfair.
    C. He was glad there were so many wounded. He hoped they would leave Boston soon.
    D. He was disappointed that he had not been in the fighting himself.

10. How did the story end?
    A. Johnny heard the Minute Men coming. He took Rab's musket and went to join them.
    B. He found Cilla and asked her to marry him before he went off to war. She agreed.
    C. Johnny saw Rab's grandfather. He started to tell him about Rab, but stopped himself.
    D. Johnny went out into the fresh air and started to whistle "Yankee Doodle."

Multiple Choice Unit Test 1 continued *Johnny Tremain*

III. Quotations
Match the quotation with the person who said it.

A. Johnny	B. Sam Adams	C. James Otis	D. Rab
E. John Hancock	F. British medical man	G. Mr. Lapham	H. Lavinia Lyte

1. 'I . . . swear from this day onward . . . to walk more humbly and modestly before God and man.'

2. 'I never do. I don't hold much with these fellows that are always trying to stir up trouble between us and England. Maybe English rule ain't always perfect, but it's good enough for me.'

3. 'It is you who put the idea in their heads. You know you usually go about with that hand in your pocket, looking as if you had an imp of Hell hidden away, and then someone asks you and you pull it out with a slow flourish, as if you said, "This is the most disgusting thing you ever saw." No wonder you scare everybody. Tonight happens you just forgot.'

4. 'Yes, God give us strength to resist. That tea cannot be allowed to land.'

5. 'You're getting above yourself--like I tried to point out to you. God is going to send you a dire punishment for your pride.'

6. 'Now boys, you forget talk like that. You remember that we don't like being here in Boston any better than you like having us. I'd rather be with my wife and children in Bath. We're both in a tight spot. But if we keep our tempers and you keep your tempers, why, we can fix things between us somehow. We're all one people, you know.'

7. 'No. This is the end. The end of one thing--the beginning of something else. They won't come back because there is going to be a war--a civil war. And we'll win. First folk like them get routed out of Milton--then out of Boston. And the cards are going to be reshuffled. Dealt again . . . Shall I shutter the kitchen too?'

8. 'No. That time is past. I will work for war: the complete freedom of these colonies from any European power. We can have that freedom only by fighting for it.'

9. 'We give all we have, lives, property, safety, skills . . . we fight, we die, for a simple thing. Only that a man can stand up.'

10. 'Isannah is going with me. Your mother has too many kittens.'

Multiple Choice Unit Test 1 continued *Johnny Tremain*

IV. Vocabulary Matching

1. apprentices
2. belligerent
3. compassionate
4. crucible
5. diffidently
6. enigmatical
7. gloating
8. grievances
9. instigated
10. invincible
11. lucid
12. paroxysm
13. piqued
14. pretense
15. repentance
16. strife
17. treason
18. trivial
19. wary
20. ethereal

A. expressing great self-satisfaction
B. a struggle or fight
C. easily understood
D. eager to fight; hostile
E. airy; fragile
F. a spasm or fit
G. sympathetic
H. betrayal of one's country
I. unpaid workers who learn a trade or craft
J. initiated; promoted the growth of
K. on guard; watchful
L. shyly; timidly
M. of little significance or value
N. felt wounded pride
O. unconquerable
P. remorse or contrition
Q. puzzling
R. a false action intended to deceive
S. a porcelain dish used for melting materials
T. reasons for protest

MULTIPLE CHOICE UNIT TEST 2 *Johnny Tremain*

I. Matching/Identification

____	1. Rab	A.	owner of *Boston Observer*
____	2. Cilla	B.	greedy merchant/Johnny's great-uncle
____	3. Lieutenant Stranger	C.	taught Johnny to ride well
____	4. Johnny Tremain	D.	treated Johnny's burned hand
____	5. Mr. Lyte	E.	said "that a man can stand up"
____	6. Sam Adams	F.	warned Lexington and Concord of battle
____	7. Paul Revere	G.	befriended Johnny and listened to his story
____	8. Dr. Warren	H.	silversmith apprentice/Observer Club messenger
____	9. Mr. Lorne	I.	said he would fight for war
____	10. James Otis	J.	Lapham daughter intended to marry Johnny

II. Multiple Choice

1. What is the setting of the novel?
    A. The novel is set in Philadelphia, Pennsylvania in 1776.
    B. The novel is set in Washington, DC. in 1864-1866.
    C. The novel is set in Boston, Massachusetts, in 1773-1775.
    D. The novel is set in San Francisco, California in 1890.

2. Which of the following statements does **not** describe Johnny's accident?
    A. Dusty gave Johnny a cracked crucible for melting the silver.
    B. As Johnny was reaching out to get the silver he slipped in beeswax that was on the floor.
    C. His right hand came down on top of the furnace, and was severely burned.
    D. When he recovered he found that the thumb and palm had drawn together, and the hand was useless.

3. Which of the following does **not** describe Johnny's looks after the accident?
    A. He wore his hat at a rakish angle.
    B. He kept his injured hand in his pocket, which made him look arrogant.
    C. His clothes were hanging off of him because he was so thin from not eating.
    D. He sometimes looked shabby and desperate.

Multiple Choice Unit Test 2 continued *Johnny Tremain*

4. Whose testimony could prove Johnny's innocence? This person was the only one who knew Johnny's story, and had heard it before he went to Mr. Lyte.
   - A. Mr. Lapham
   - B. Rab
   - C. Isannah
   - D. Cilla

5. What job did Johnny take?
   - A. He became a waiter at the African Queen.
   - B. He delivered papers for the *Boston Observer*.
   - C. He began studying law with Josiah Quincy.
   - D. He became the town crier.

6. What was the grievance the colonists had with England in the Fall of 1773?
   - A. There was a tax on tea. The colonists insisted they would not be taxed if they could not vote for the men who taxed them.
   - B. The people were not allowed to worship as they pleased. They all had to belong to the Church of England.
   - C. All mail in and out of Boston was inspected by the British soldiers. The colonist said this was an invasion of their privacy.
   - D. All boys over the age of thirteen had to go to England to serve in the Army. The townspeople didn't want their young men to go.

7. Which of the following did **not** happen on the night of December 16?
   - A. The men and boys disguised themselves as Indians.
   - B. They damaged all of the cargo on the ships, not just the tea.
   - C. Many people stood on the shore watching.
   - D. Admiral Montague shouted from a window that they would all have to pay the fiddler.

8. What happened because Johnny passed on the information from Lydia?
   - A. John Hancock avoided being arrested.
   - B. The Minute Men captured a whole regiment of British soldiers.
   - C. Paul Revere warned the men in Portsmouth and they seized the British stores.
   - D. The Revolutionary War began.

Multiple Choice Unit Test 2 continued *Johnny Tremain*

9. What was Johnny's observation as he watched the boats full of wounded British soldiers being unloaded?
    - A. He thought the bloodshed was a terrible waste of lives on both sides.
    - B. The wounded officers and privates were treated differently. He thought this was unfair.
    - C. He was glad there were so many wounded. He hoped they would leave Boston soon.
    - D. He was disappointed that he had not been in the fighting himself.

10. How did the story end?
    - A. Johnny heard the Minute Men coming. He took Rab's musket and went to join them.
    - B. He found Cilla and asked her to marry him before he went off to war. She agreed.
    - C. Johnny saw Rab's grandfather. He started to tell him about Rab, but stopped himself.
    - D. Johnny went out into the fresh air and started to whistle "Yankee Doodle."

Multiple Choice Unit Test 2 continued *Johnny Tremain*

III. Quotations

Match the quotation with the person who said it.

A. Johnny Tremain   B. Sam Adams   C. James Otis   D. Rab
E. Mr. Lorne   F. Mrs. Lapham   G. Dr. Warren   H. Lavinia Lyte

1. "My! That's worse than anything I had imagined. Now isn't that a shame! Bright boy like Johnny just ruined. No more good than a horse with sprung knees.'

2. 'It's about like dancing . . . keeping rhythm. You'll learn right off. Of course you'll be scared, but just remember this: no matter how scared you are, he's more so.'

3. 'Without you, there would not have been any belief in liberty to lose. I will, as always, do anything--everything you wish.'

4. 'We give all we have, lives, property, safety, skills . . . we fight, we die, for a simple thing. Only that a man can stand up.'

5. 'You know, my father had to fly France because of the tyranny over there. He was only a child. But now, in a way, I'm fighting for that child . . . that no frightened lost child ever is sent out a refugee from his own country because of race or religion.'

6. 'Miss Lavinia is about making a monkey out of Isannah.'

7. 'Isannah is going with me. Your mother has too many kittens.'

8. 'It is just as James Otis said. We are fighting, partly, for just that. Because a man is a private is no reason he should be treated like cordwood.'

9. 'You can have that musket. I sort of like to think of its going on. I've put a better stock on it, changed the angle of the steel. Look at that flint. The one it had was too smooth. I've knapped it.'

10. 'Yes, and some if us would die--so other men can stand up on their feet like men. A great many are going to die for that. They have in the past. They will a hundred years from now--two hundred. God grant there will always be good enough. Men like Rab.'

Multiple Choice Unit Test 2 continued *Johnny Tremain*

IV. Vocabulary Matching

1. apoplectic
2. arrogantly
3. berated
4. civil
5. demeanor
6. disperse
7. fatuous
8. imperceptibly
9. instigated
10. indolent
11. lamentably
12. martial
13. oratory
14. prodigiously
15. punctilious
16. seditious
17. tediously
18. tyranny
19. surfeited
20. wavered

A. the way in which a person behaves
B. loss of muscular control and consciousness
C. in a slow and boring manner
D. enormously
E. regrettably
F. incited; promoted the growth of
G. showed indecision
H. to scatter in different directions
I. precise; scrupulous
J. relating to citizens
K. saturated; over-filled
L. rebuked
M. boastfully
N. public speaking
O. unjust use of absolute power
P. not understandable
Q. rebellious
R. unconsciously foolish
S. relating to war
T. habitually lazy

ANSWER SHEET   Multiple Choice Unit Tests   *Johnny Tremain*

I. Matching	III. Quotations	IV. Vocabulary
1. _____	1. _____	1. _____
2. _____	2. _____	2. _____
3. _____	3. _____	3. _____
4. _____	4. _____	4. _____
5. _____	5. _____	5. _____
6. _____	6. _____	6. _____
7. _____	7. _____	7. _____
8. _____	8. _____	8. _____
9. _____	9. _____	9. _____
10. _____	10. _____	10. _____
		11. _____
		12. _____
		13. _____
		14. _____
		15. _____
		16. _____
		17. _____
		18. _____
		19. _____
		20. _____

II. Multiple Choice

1. (A) (B) (C) (D)
2. (A) (B) (C) (D)
3. (A) (B) (C) (D)
4. (A) (B) (C) (D)
5. (A) (B) (C) (D)
6. (A) (B) (C) (D)
7. (A) (B) (C) (D)
8. (A) (B) (C) (D)
9. (A) (B) (C) (D)
10. (A) (B) (C) (D)

ANSWER SHEET KEY   Multiple Choice Unit Test 1 *Johnny Tremain*

I. Matching	III. Quotations	IV. Vocabulary
1. E	1. A	1. I
2. A	2. E	2. D
3. D	3. D	3. G
4. J	4. B	4. S
5. F	5. G	5. L
6. B	6. F	6. Q
7. H	7. A	7. A
8. C	8. B	8. T
9. I	9. C	9. J
10. G	10. H	10. O
		11. C
		12. F
		13. N
		14. R
		15. P
		16. B
		17. H
		18. M
		19. K
		20. E

II. Multiple Choice

1. ( ) (B) (C) (D)
2. (A) (B) (C) ( )
3. ( ) (B) (C) (D)
4. (A) (B) (C) ( )
5. (A) (B) ( ) (D)
6. ( ) (B) (C) (D)
7. (A) (B) (C) ( )
8. ( ) (B) (C) (D)
9. (A) ( ) (C) (D)
10. (A) (B) ( ) (D)

ANSWER SHEET KEY   Multiple Choice Unit Test 2 *Johnny Tremain*

I. Matching	III. Quotations	IV. Vocabulary
1. G	1. F	1. B
2. J	2. D	2. M
3. C	3. E	3. L
4. H	4. C	4. J
5. B	5. B	5. A
6. I	6. A	6. H
7. F	7. H	7. R
8. D	8. A	8. P
9. A	9. D	9. F
10. E	10. G	10. T
		11. E
		12. S
		13. N
		14. D
		15. I
		16. Q
		17. C
		18. O
		19. K
		20. G

II. Multiple Choice

1. (A) (B) ( ) (D)
2. ( ) (B) (C) (D)
3. (A) (B) ( ) (D)
4. (A) (B) (C) ( )
5. (A) ( ) (C) (D)
6. ( ) (B) (C) (D)
7. (A) ( ) (C) (D)
8. (A) (B) ( ) (D)
9. (A) ( ) (C) (D)
10. (A) (B) ( ) (D)

UNIT RESOURCES

BULLETIN BOARD IDEAS *Johnny Tremain*

1. Save one corner of the board for the best of students' *Johnny Tremain* writing assignments. You may want to use background maps of Boston and colonial America to represent the setting of the novel.

2. Take one of the word search puzzles from the extra activities packet and with a marker copy it over in a large size on the bulletin board. Write the clue words you find to one side. Invite students prior to and after class to find the words and circle them on the bulletin board.

3. Have students find or draw pictures that they think resemble the people in the book.

4. Invite students to help make an interactive bulletin board quiz. Give each student a half-sheet of paper (about 4"x5") folded in half so that it can open. On the outside flap, have each student write a description of one of the characters in the text. On the inside, they will write the name of the character. You can staple or tack these papers to the bulletin board so that the students can read the descriptions and lift the flaps to find the answers.

5. Collect pictures of the area mentioned in the book.

6. Have students draw book jackets for *Johnny Tremain* and display them.

7. Have students make posters opposing the tea tax and display them on the bulletin board.

8. Display articles about the Revolutionary War, especially the earliest battles in and around Boston.

9. Have students design postcards depicting the settings of the book.

10. Display a large map of the Boston area and have students mark the route that the British soldiers took during the first battles. Also mark the routes that Paul Revere and Billy Dawes took to warn Lexington and Concord. The Boston Chamber of commerce or a travel agency may be able to supply some maps of the historic area of Boston. Students could locate the wharf, Paul Revere's house, Boston Common, and other areas mentioned in the book.

EXTRA ACTIVITIES *Johnny Tremain*

One of the difficulties in teaching a novel is that all students don't read at the same speed. One student who likes to read may take the book home and finish it in a day or two. Sometimes a few students finish the in-class assignments early. The problem, then, is finding suitable extra activities for students.

One thing that helps is to keep a little library in the classroom. For this unit on *Johnny Tremain* you might check out from the school or public library other books by Esther Forbes. There are also many other historical fiction novels dealing with the American Revolution that students would enjoy reading.

Your students who have reading difficulties, or speak English as a second language may benefit from listening to all or part of the book on tape. It is available commercially, or you could have a parent or a few students with good oral reading skills make a tape.

Other things you may keep on hand are word search puzzles. Several puzzles relating directly to *Johnny Tremain* are included in the unit. Feel free to duplicate them.

Some students may like to draw. You might devise a contest or allow some extra-credit grade for students who draw characters or scenes from *Johnny Tremain.* Note, too, that if the students do not want to keep their drawings you may pick up some extra bulletin board materials this way. If you have a contest and you supply the prize. You could, possibly, make the drawing itself a non-refundable entry fee.

Give students several options for independent projects. These could be developed from the whole book or a chapter, depending on your time and your students' abilities. Some suggestions are: writing a play; performing a skit; creating a puppet show; writing a Reader's Theater play; making a diorama; making chapter or story maps; re-writing the story as a picture book for younger students; writing a song about the book; doing arts and crafts related to the book.

Have maps, a globe, and travel brochures on hand for easy reference. Travel agencies and automobile clubs are good sources for these materials.

The pages which follow contain games, puzzles, and worksheets. The keys, when appropriate, immediately follow the puzzle or worksheet. There are two main groups of activities: one group for the unit; that is, generally relating to the *Johnny Tremain* text, and another group of activities related strictly to the *Johnny Tremain* vocabulary.

Directions for the games, puzzles, and worksheets are self-explanatory. The object here is to provide you with extra materials you may use in any way you choose.

MORE ACTIVITIES

1. Pick one of the incidents for students to dramatize. Encourage students to write dialog for the characters. (Perhaps you could assign various stories to different groups of students so more than one story could be acted and more students could participate.)

2. Have students design a book cover (front and back and inside flaps) for *Johnny Tremain*.

3. Have students design a bulletin board (ready to be put up; not just sketched) for *Johnny Tremain*.

4. Invite a story teller to tell one or more stories related to *Johnny Tremain* to the class.

5. Use some of the related topics (noted earlier for an in-class library) as topics for research, reports, or written papers, or as topics for guest speakers.

6. Help students design and produce a talk show. Choose one of the story incidents as the topic. The host will interview the various characters. (Students should make up the questions they want the host to ask the characters.)

7. Have students work in pairs to create an interview with one of the characters. One student should be the interviewer and the other should be the interviewee. Students can work together to compose questions for the interviewer to ask. Each pair of students could present their interview to the class.

8. Invite students who have read other books by Esther Forbes to present book talks to the class.

9. Invite students who have read a biographical sketch of Esther Forbes to tell the class about her life.

10. Contact a local historical society or the history department of a university to find an authority on the Revolutionary War. Invite the person to speak to the class.

11. If you live in or near an area that performs Revolutionary War battle re-enactments, you may want to take the students to see one.

12. Historical museums may have traveling exhibits that they will loan to you, or take the students on a trip to a museum to see a colonial era display.

13. Invite someone who has lived in one of the areas mentioned in the book to speak to the class.

14. Have students hold small group discussions related to topics in the book. Assign a recorder and a speaker for each group. Have the speaker from each group make a report to the class.

15. It is not clear what happened to Johnny Tremain. Have students work in small groups to write a sequel telling what he did next.

16. Encourage students to use the Internet (with adult supervision) to find out more information about the Revolutionary War.

17. Watch a video or laser disc presentation about colonial America or the Revolutionary War.

WORD SEARCH *Johnny Tremain*

All the words in this list are associated with *Johnny Tremain* with emphasis on the characters and events being studied in the unit. The words are placed backwards, forward, diagonally, up and down. The words used in the puzzle are listed below.

```
Y T G J S N W O T S E L R A H C K B J L E E H A E A B A H D W Q L T Y
R C O N C D B G D S U O G R W F X T X E N I A C U Z W A V M A D G E C
Z F F M I B U B K N K T U T Q Z B S Q G S J N F G Q L T B L V W U Y H
W A Y Y U B N L R E L I N H G A P I L H C T N C Y D X T M K H M R Y L
T T A U T V D I E V P S L I A R S A Z G J M A G X Y S V Y L L Q W S L
T K N S L E C I D A P F F I D P N C O E K R S Y D E K G D L G U Y C G
G H H N Q G V C P J M C B J X D B J B H V D I N H I Y J T W C S O I N
R U U Z K V U L F I S B M N U V N B Q T G C O G F F A U G G T S Y T I
E V P K R Z L U P I K O W K J R Z W Z Y V C V V K J C M B Z I I F M K
E G F X D N M T L Y F K X R A Q A G D R W A R R E N P S U Y D R I Z P
N O F W K I U V X V S F F H M P H B J Z B Y N Z H G O T N K C T C M M
D H T W I Z E W G R H Z V K S U B M Q S U F W T F M O O E W R G P Y U
R H Q O K R L C X O R G I V D T V D T E G O J K D Y D N O L K I W I P
A O U Y S D E M J Q A J H S S E M I I B W F Q R K N P V Y S O X C Y K
G R M M C A K B E I U D C R G T K I J R S T Y K P T M T E A H L O J O
O Y I J Q C Z K N U M P J Z X H H S G O P J E Q H A E S A W J A W P A
N T J M R O X I H A G V B F M L Z U F F O T W R A B F E G G U U Y D Q
H S J A E B V J I U F A G Z S W G M C R D B V A S G G E V A W A W B H
K I M W Y A D K N I S Z T F C S S N E E U Q C I R F A I R Z W F K M E
K M M P L L E X I N G T O N D E W F K H C B O S T O N S N W A T Y T I
E L D O O D E E K N A Y X J O T K X P T Z N I D O K G S D G P O B I Q
V T V C D X S Y M P S M D L G M A U E S M N R U L Y U E V L N C J P S
X K D B S W T V Y Y E S D T J S O F W E Q F W Z R E P B Q N P O T W L
```

MONTAGUE	ENGLAND	LYTE
AFRIC QUEEN	ISANNAH	GREEN DRAGON
BESSIE	OTIS	YANKEE DOODLE
BOSTON	MADGE	RAB
CHARLESTOWN	PUMPKIN	SILVERSMITH
LEXINGTON	TEA	ESTHER FORBES
DR WARREN	LAVINIA	

CROSSWORD *Johnny Tremain*

CROSSWORD CLUES *Johnny Tremain*

ACROSS
1 Pretended to be drunk to leave the city
4 Gave Johnny a broken crucible
5 Setting of the novel
8 Took supplies from Charlestown
10 Lapham daughter intended to marry Johnny
12 Attracted many because of her frail nature
13 Where the tea was thrown: Boston ___
14 Greedy merchant: Jonathan ___
16 Main speaker at Observer Club meetings
20 First to hear Johnny's story
22 Warned Lexington and Concord of battle
23 Hung the lanterns in Christ Church
25 Apprentice who was afraid of Johnny
28 Preached more about politics than God
29 Said "that a man can stand up"
30 Owned *Boston Observer*
32 Colonial army: ___ Men
33 Silversmith from Baltimore: Percival ___
34 Gave his musket to Johnny
35 Popular Boston restaurant: Afric ___

DOWN
1 Daughter of Liberty
2 Owned silversmith shop
3 Owner of the colonies
4 Patriotic song: Yankee ___
6 Colonists refused to pay tax on it
7 Town near Lexington
9 Johnny's horse
10 General Gage took the cannon and gunpowder from there
11 Meeting place for artisans in spy network: Green ___
15 They were loyal to England
17 Married a British soldier
18 Ran off with Frizel, Junior
21 Wealthy merchant, ordered sugar basin from Mr. Lapham
24 Treated Johnny's burned hand
26 Author
27 Site of first shot of Revolutionary War
29 Silversmith apprentice turned rebel
30 Johnny's father: Dr. Charles ___
31 In charge of British troops at battle in Lexington

CROSSWORD ANSWER KEY *Johnny Tremain*

MATCHING QUIZ *Johnny Tremain*

Directions: Place the letter of the matching definition on the blank line.

_____	1. Billy Dawes	A.	Johnny's wild horse
_____	2. Charlestown	B.	fixed Johnny's injured hand
_____	3. Colonel Smith	C.	Gage took its cannons and gunpowder
_____	4. Dove	D.	attracted many because of her frail nature
_____	5. Dr. Warren	E.	gave Johnny a broken crucible
_____	6. Dusty	F.	in charge of British at Lexington
_____	7. Goblin	G.	town near Lexington
_____	8. Green Dragon	H.	organized spy ring
_____	9. James Otis	I.	liked having Johnny as a riding pupil
_____	10. John Hancock	J.	said he would fight for war
_____	11. Lavinia Lyte	K.	gave Johnny is musket when he died
_____	12. Mrs. Lapham	L.	owner of Boston Observer
_____	13. Mr. Lorne	M.	apprentice who was afraid of Johnny
_____	14. Rab	N.	helped clarify reason for the rebellion
_____	15. Sam Adams	O.	meeting place for spying artisans
_____	16. Paul Revere	P.	finally married Mr. Tweedie
_____	17. Lieutenant Stranger	Q.	pretended to be drunk to leave the city
_____	18. Isannah	R.	author of *Johnny Tremain*
_____	19. Esther Forbes	S.	made Isannah her protégée
_____	20. Concord	T.	wealthy merchant and Whig leader

ANSWER KEY MATCHING QUIZ *Johnny Tremain*

Directions: Place the letter of the matching definition on the blank line.

Answer	#	Term		Letter	Definition
Q	1.	Billy Dawes		A.	Johnny's wild horse
C	2.	Charlestown		B.	fixed Johnny's injured hand
F	3.	Colonel Smith		C.	Gage took its cannons and gunpowder
E	4.	Dove		D.	attracted many because of her frail nature
B	5.	Dr. Warren		E.	gave Johnny a broken crucible
M	6.	Dusty		F.	in charge of British at Lexington
A	7.	Goblin		G.	town near Lexington
O	8.	Green Dragon		H.	organized spy ring
N	9.	James Otis		I.	liked having Johnny as a riding pupil
T	10.	John Hancock		J.	said he would fight for war
S	11.	Lavinia Lyte		K.	gave Johnny is musket when he died
P	12.	Mrs. Lapham		L.	owner of Boston Observer
L	13.	Mr. Lorne		M.	apprentice who was afraid of Johnny
K	14.	Rab		N.	helped clarify reason for the rebellion
J	15.	Sam Adams		O.	meeting place for spying artisans
H	16.	Paul Revere		P.	finally married Mr. Tweedie
I	17.	Lieutenant Stranger		Q.	pretended to be drunk to leave the city
D	18.	Isannah		R.	author of *Johnny Tremain*
R	19.	Esther Forbes		S.	made Isannah her protégée
G	20.	Concord		T.	wealthy merchant and Whig leader

MATCHING QUIZ 2 *Johnny Tremain*

Directions: Place the letter of the matching definition on the blank line.

____	1. Admiral Montague	A.	hung the lanterns in Christ Church
____	2. Bessie	B.	fixed Johnny's injured hand
____	3. Boston	C.	religious owner of silver shop
____	4. Cilla	D.	Lapham who intended to marry Johnny
____	5. Dorcas	E.	colonists refused to pay tax on it
____	6. Madge	F.	Boston tavern for wealthier customers
____	7. Dr. Warren	G.	setting of novel
____	8. Dr. Latour	H.	married a British soldier
____	9. Green Dragon	I.	ran off with Frizel, Jr.
____	10. Josiah Quincy	J.	greedy merchant & Johnny's great uncle
____	11. Mr. Lapham	K.	said citizens would pay the fiddler
____	12. Pumpkin	L.	meeting place for spying artisans
____	13. Rev. Sam Cooper	M.	leaders of revolt against England
____	14. Robert Newman	N.	gave British news to the Whigs
____	15. Johnny Tremain	O.	Daughter of Liberty
____	16. Sons of Liberty	P.	traded his musket for country clothes
____	17. Afric Queen	Q.	defended Johnny in court for free
____	18. tea	R.	Johnny's father
____	19. Jonathan Lyte	S.	preached more about politics than God
____	20. *Boston Observer*	T.	newspaper that printed treasonous news

ANSWER KEY MATCHING QUIZ 2 *Johnny Tremain*

K	1.	Admiral Montague	A.	hung the lanterns in Christ Church
O	2.	Bessie	B.	fixed Johnny's injured hand
G	3.	Boston	C.	religious owner of silver shop
D	4.	Cilla	D.	Lapham who intended to marry Johnny
I	5.	Dorcas	E.	colonists refused to pay tax on it
H	6	Madge	F.	Boston tavern for wealthier customers
B	7.	Dr. Warren	G.	setting of novel
R	8.	Dr. Latour	H.	married a British soldier
L	9.	Green Dragon	I.	ran off with Frizel, Jr.
Q	10.	Josiah Quincy	J.	greedy merchant & Johnny's great uncle
C	11.	Mr. Lapham	K.	said citizens would pay the fiddler
P	12.	Pumpkin	L.	meeting place for spying artisans
S	13.	Rev. Sam Cooper	M.	leaders of revolt against England
A	14.	Robert Newman	N.	gave British news to the Whigs
N	15.	Johnny Tremain	O.	Daughter of Liberty
M	16.	Sons of Liberty	P.	traded his musket for country clothes
F	17.	Afric Queen	Q.	defended Johnny in court for free
E	18.	tea	R.	Johnny's father
J	19.	Jonathan Lyte	S.	preached more about politics than God
T	20.	*Boston Observer*	T.	newspaper that printed treasonous news

JUGGLE LETTER REVIEW GAME *Johnny Tremain*

SCRAMBLED	**WORD**	**CLUE**
OUNAMGET	MONTAGUE	said citizens would pay the fiddler
AEFIRUCENQ	AFRIC QUEEN	popular Boston restaurant
EESBSI	BESSIE	daughter of liberty
ESWAD	DAWES	pretend to be drunk to leave the city
OONSTB	BOSTON	setting of novel
ARHORB	HARBOR	where the tea was thrown
BOREVERS	OBSERVER	newspaper that printed articles about revolt
ILCAL	CILLA	liked Johnny's last name with her first
HSITM	SMITH	British colonel at Lexington
NOOCRDC	CONCORD	town near Lexington
VODE	DOVE	gave Johnny a broken crucible
LOUART	LATOUR	Johnny's father
ERWANR	WARREN	treated Johnny's burned hand
LNANGDE	ENGLAND	owner of the colonies
GLINOB	GOBLIN	Johnny's horse
DERENRAGONG	GREEN DRAGON	meeting place for artisans in spy network
IANAHNS	ISANNAH	attracted many because of her frail nature
HCONCKA	HANCOCK	wealthy Whig merchant
ITARMEN	TREMAIN	silversmith apprentice-turned rebel
TELY	LYTE	greedy merchant
NQICUY	QUINCY	lawyer who defended Johnny for free
NAVIIAL	LAVINIA	made Isannah her protégée
GINXTOLNE	LEXINGTON	site of first shot of Revolutionary War
RSRAGENT	STRANGER	taught Johnny to ride a horse well
DGEAM	MADGE	married a British soldier
MNUEENITM	MINUTE MEN	colonial army
LMPHAA	LAPHAM	made original sugar basin and set
ORLEN	LORNE	owner of Boston Observer
EVERRE	REVERE	warned Lexington and Concord of battle
DTEEIEW	TWEEDIE	silversmith from Baltimore
MPUKIPN	PUMPKIN	gave his musket to Johnny
BAR	RAB	first to hear Johnny's story
OCROPE	COOPER	preached more about politics than God
ANEMWN	NEWMAN	hung the lanterns in Christ Church
SAAMD	ADAMS	main speaker at Observer Club meetings
ISILMERSTHV	SILVERSMITH	Johnny's first occupation
OIESTR	TORIES	loyal to England
GWISH	WHIGS	wanted freedom from England

VOCABULARY RESOURCES

VOCABULARY WORD SEARCH

All the words in this list are associated with *Johnny Tremain* with emphasis on the vocabulary words being studied in the unit. The words are placed backwards, forward, diagonally, up and down. The clues below the word search will help identify the word.

```
M H A V Y J F Y I R S W B T J Y L J P T C P Y O V Y F P L U K O J U Q
N T V M I A R R U R G Q M K Q F T I N R U O L Z X C O B K O V X D B R
J I Y I K A B Y L T N E G I L I D E R N O M M U N E F T B L T U O C D
N E V N T E H L B P W N I L K B R N C E P D S P S M W D A W M A M I T
J R D I M C U Y R B O N A D O E W T K T P F I D A W I B M B D Q P L E
S V L H U C X O A I Z I G W G B I T N E R D J G E S A R Q Q K Q N O Z
X O I X I J M V T A T D C I I L H E P O O U C E I T S Y R O N P D L G
S D K D T E T C Y R M Q L A I B L L Y K T G C N E O R I Q N M O P N Q
R H D D N E E P A Y Y L F O D U W A I O E L H D D X U M O Y D T M E I
B B N A E R N M J R E D U K B L P I L K G T W Z H T P S G N O H V H O
K N D I R T X T F B D S S R W U N V X P E I X K G E U T L C A P A B K
A E I U S H P L A M F U U M R F B I I J E Z Z N T U E S L Y M T P M X
U R S K C A E C I T U T W D G B W R U A T M V E A O B H M A I T E Y N
Z N R N O B X O D D I N K G L O A T I N G D O I Y S I C R L J Z M L W
I X V O S T L V M H I V D R G N N R K C P N M F G P K D I E A F K Z Q
E K P G G M P H H K V L E A S V Y E R H A L S J A F E V O G U U U Q K
E H W D Q A D R A G G A L L N D N V P K U E E T H N I S C Q I R Q P M
F F I V M O N T L G E G T L Y E N E K Q V H W N T C M U F L A C C I D
Z P I O K G F T V B E R A T E D A R M N N S E N I I Q L I V Y O O F M
H B K R E M I W L V M F H T Q F C T L O P E M A N E A I I K N H K V I
I I R F T H U X Q Y S Y N A B U R E U I C A H N O C N P J E F Z D J L
C S V T P S D W Z H T M A K L E K D M S P M Z F F J L T D N U E A G M
```

DILIGENTLY	MARTIAL	COMPASSIONATE
PRODIGIOUSLY	PUNCTILIOUS	FLACCID
TURBULENT	PERIL	ARROGANTLY
CIVIL	LENIENT	MUNDANE
CANNY	LAGGARD	ABATED
LUCID	INSURRECTION	BERATED
TRIVIAL	PROTEGEE	PROMENADE
SOLITARY	TENTATIVELY	REVERTED
ARDENT	GLOATING	BELLIGERENT
QUALMS	BELFRY	STRIFE

VOCABULARY CROSSWORD *Johnny Tremain*

VOCABULARY CROSSWORD CLUES *Johnny Tremain*

ACROSS
1 Passionate; displaying a strong enthusiasm
6 Bell tower
7 Those who work in return for instruction
9 Rebellious
12 Merciful; indulgent
14 Unconsciously foolish
17 Having loss of muscular control and sensation
19 On guard; watchful
21 Lacking vigor or energy
22 A supply of weapons
24 Reverence
25 Reduced in amount
26 A struggle or fight
27 Ordinary; boring
28 Easily understood; intelligible

DOWN
1 Turned away
2 Hated
3 Betrayal of one's country
4 Uproar
5 Awaken or excite
6 Trading goods or services without money
7 Ghost
8 Danger
10 The way in which a person behaves
11 Rebuked; scolded; put down
13 Unconcerned or indifferent
15 Relating to a citizen
16 Food or beverage made of mixed ingredients
17 Boastfully
18 Careful and shrewd
19 Showed indecision
20 Relating to public speaking
23 Unjust use of absolute power
24 Felt wounded pride

VOCABULARY CROSSWORD ANSWER KEY *Johnny Tremain*

VOCABULARY WORKSHEET 1

Directions: Place the letter of the matching definition on the blank line.

____ 1.	promenade	A.	a public place for walking
____ 2.	imperceptibly	B.	promoted the growth of; incited
____ 3.	reverted	C.	of little significance or value
____ 4.	apparition	D.	merciful; indulgent
____ 5.	enigmatical	E.	returned to a former condition
____ 6.	fatuous	F.	overwhelmed; swamped
____ 7.	treason	G.	precise; scrupulous
____ 8.	instigated	H.	to appease; to make concessions
____ 9.	demeanor	I.	the way in which a person behaves
____ 10.	inundated	J.	hardly noticed
____ 11.	prodigiously	K.	impressively great; enormously
____ 12.	wavered	L.	a ghostly figure
____ 13.	civil	M.	uneasy feelings
____ 14.	loitering	N.	unconsciously foolish
____ 15.	placate	O.	standing idly by
____ 16.	trivial	P.	puzzling
____ 17.	qualms	Q.	passionate; displaying strong emotions
____ 18.	ardent	R.	showed indecision
____ 19.	punctilious	S.	betrayal of one's country
____ 20.	lenient	T.	relating to a citizen

ANSWER KEY VOCABULARY WORKSHEET 1

Directions: Place the letter of the matching definition on the blank line.

A	1.	promenade	A.	a public place for walking
J	2.	imperceptibly	B.	promoted the growth of; incited
E	3.	reverted	C.	of little significance or value
L	4.	apparition	D.	merciful; indulgent
P	5.	enigmatical	E.	returned to a former condition
N	6.	fatuous	F.	overwhelmed; swamped
S	7.	treason	G.	precise; scrupulous
B	8.	instigated	H.	to appease; to make concessions
I	9.	demeanor	I.	the way in which a person behaves
F	10.	inundated	J.	hardly noticed
K	11.	prodigiously	K.	impressively great; enormously
R	12.	wavered	L.	a ghostly figure
T	13.	civil	M.	uneasy feelings
O	14.	loitering	N.	unconsciously foolish
H	15.	placate	O.	standing idly by
C	16.	trivial	P.	puzzling
M	17.	qualms	Q.	passionate; displaying strong emotions
Q	18.	ardent	R.	showed indecision
G	19.	punctilious	S.	betrayal of one's country
D	20.	lenient	T.	relating to a citizen

VOCABULARY WORKSHEET 2

1. **misbeliever**
   A. apoplectic   B. apprentices   C. heretic   D. poultice

2. **expressing self-satisfaction**
   mundane   B. piety   C. wary   D. gloating

3. **a bell tower**
   A. belfry   B. belligerent   C. promenade   D. clamor

4. **sympathetic**
   A. demeanor   B. oratory   C. compassionate   D. piqued

5. **lacking in vigor or energy**
   A. turbulent   B. flaccid   C. lucid   D. canny

6. **bulging out**
   A. loitering   B. solitary   C. punctilious   D. protuberant

7. **boastfully**
   A. disconsolately   B. arrogantly   C. tentatively   D. tediously

8. **ordinary**
   A. indolent   B. wary   C. mundane   D. enigmatical

9. **found fault with**
   A. seditious   B. reproved   C. detested   D. instigated

10. **eager to fight; hostile**
    A. lamentable   B. incapacity   C. lucid   D. belligerent

11. **turned away**
    A. averted   B. loitering   C. dilapidated   D. subdued

12. **hardly noticed**
    A. lenient   B. laggard   C. imperceptibly   D. invincible

13. **in a friendly manner**
    A. surfeited   B. arsenal   C. gloating   D. cordially

14. **puzzling**
    A. parasitic   B. enigmatical   C. apoplectic   D. berated

15. **unconcerned; indifferent**
    A. abated   B. nonchalant   C. indolent   D. seditious

16. **a false action intended to deceive**
    A. treason   B. repentance   C. pretense   D. demeanor

17. **uproar**
    A. arouse   B. clamor   C. oratory   D. indenture

18. **reasons for protest**
    A. qualms   B. trivial   C. arsenal   D. grievances

19. **spasm or fit**
    A. concoction   B. paroxysm   C. peril   D. protégée

20. **trading without money**
    A. bartering   B. instigating   C. insurrection   D. loitering

ANSWER KEY VOCABULARY WORKSHEET 2

C 1. **misbeliever**
   A. apoplectic   B. apprentices   C. **heretic**   D. poultice

D 2. **expressing self-satisfaction**
   A. mundane   B. piety   C. wary   D. **gloating**

A 3. **a bell tower**
   A. **belfry**   B. belligerent   C. promenade   D. clamor

C 4. **sympathetic**
   A. demeanor   B. oratory   C. **compassionate**   D. piqued

B 5. **lacking in vigor or energy**
   A. turbulent   B. **flaccid**   C. lucid   D. canny

D 6. **bulging out**
   A. loitering   B. solitary   C. punctilious   D. **protuberant**

B 7. **boastfully**
   A. disconsolately   **B. arrogantly**   C. tentatively   D. tediously

C 8. **ordinary**
   A. indolent   B. wary   C. **mundane**   D. enigmatical

B 9. **found fault with**
   A. seditious   B. **reproved**   C. detested   D. instigated

D 10. **eager to fight; hostile**
   A. lamentable   B. incapacity   C. lucid   D. **belligerent**

A 11. **turned away**
   A. **averted**   B. loitering   C. dilapidated   D. subdued

C 12. **hardly noticed**
   A. lenient   B. laggard   C. **imperceptibly**   D. invincible

D 13. **in a friendly manner**
   A. surfeited   B. arsenal   C. gloating   D. **cordially**

B 14. **puzzling**
   A. parasitic   B. **enigmatical**   C. apoplectic   D. berated

B 15. **unconcerned; indifferent**
   A. abated   B. **nonchalant**   C. indolent   D. seditious

C. 16. **a false action intended to deceive**
   A. treason   B. repentance   C. **pretense**   D. demeanor

B 17. **uproar**
   A. arouse   B. **clamor**   C. oratory   D. indenture

D 18. **reasons for protest**
   A. qualms   B. trivial   C. arsenal   D. **grievances**

B 19. **spasm or fit**
   A. concoction   B. **paroxysm**   C. peril   D. protégée

A 20. **trading without money**
   A. **bartering**   B. instigating   C. insurrection   D. loitering

VOCABULARY JUGGLE LETTER REVIEW GAME
Johnny Tremain

WORD	**CLUE**	
BATEDA	ABATED	reduced in amount
RAENTD	ARDENT	passionate; displaying strong enthusiasm
SAUEOR	AROUSE	awaken or excite
RASALEN	ARSENAL	a supply of weapons
ATEREDV	AVERTED	turned away
TBNAERRIG	BARTERING	trading goods or services without money
YBFELR	BELFRY	a bell tower
EDREABT	BERATED	rebuked; scolded
NANCY	CANNY	careful and shrewd
LIVCI	CIVIL	relating to a citizen
MOACRL	CLAMOR	uproar
OLRDYCIAL	CORDIALLY	sincerely
BRUILECC	CRUCIBLE	a porcelain dish used for melting silver
TUIVCATEL	CULTIVATE	to nurture; foster
ESETEDTD	DETESTED	hated
IRPEDSES	DISPERSE	scatter in different directions.
UUSTFOA	FATUOUS	unconsciously foolish
LCACFID	FLACCID	lacking vigor or energy
LTOGAIGN	GLOATING	expressing self-satisfaction
HTICREE	HERETIC	misbeliever
NAIPYACCIT	INCAPACITY	inadequate strength or ability
IUNTDEREN	INDENTURE	unpaid service to another
NISIATTEDG	INSTIGATED	promoted the growth of; initiated
IDNUETNDA	INUNDATED	overwhelmed; swamped
LAGGARD	LAGGARD	hanging back or falling behind
ELNIENTN	LENIENT	merciful; indulgent
TLOERIING	LOITERING	standing idly about; lingering aimlessly
UIDLC	LUCID	easily understood; intelligible
MIATLRA	MARTIAL	relating to war
DUNMANE	MUNDANE	ordinary
ROTORYA	ORATORY	public speaking
EILRP	PERIL	imminent danger
ITPYE	PIETY	reverence
QIUPED	PIQUED	felt wounded pride
CPALATE	PLACATE	to appease; make concessions
OLTIUCPE	POULTICE	dressing for a wound or injury
PETESERN	PRETENSE	a false action intended to deceive

ULAMQS	QUALMS	uneasy feelings
REPOEVRD	REPROVED	found fault with
TREVEERD	REVERTED	returned to a former condition
YASLOITR	SOLITARY	alone
SERIFT	STRIFE	a struggle or fight
UDUESDB	SUBDUED	brought under control; quieted
RATSOEN	TREASON	betrayal of one's country
ARIVTIL	TRIVIAL	of little significance or value
AWRY	WARY	on guard; watchful
AVRWEED	WAVERED	showed indecision

www.ingramcontent.com/pod-product-compliance
Lightning Source LLC
Chambersburg PA
CBHW051409070526
44584CB00023B/3348